Lying Spirit

Lying Spirit: What Man Sees Versus What God Says
Copyright © 2022 Herr Speights Ventures, LLC

NorDrey Books is an imprint of Herr Speights Ventures, LLC. All rights reserved. Produced and printed in the United States of America. Except for brief quotations embodied in critical articles and reviews, no person or entity may reproduce any part of this book in any form, electronic or mechanical, including information storage and retrieval systems, without written permission from an authorized representative of the copyright holder, Herr Speights Ventures, LLC, which reserves all rights not necessarily mentioned herein. See www.HerrSpeightsVentures.com for contact information and other details.

FIRST EDITION

Lying Spirit:
What Man Sees Versus What God Says
Speights, M. Richard

photographs, graphics, layout, and design
by M. Richard Speights—1st ed.

ISBN: 979-8-9860796-0-8 Paperback
ISBN: 979-8-9860796-1-5 Ebook
Religion

NorDrey Books
Missoula, Montana

This is For Patricia Ann Herren

Christian
Artist
Author
Teacher
Missionary
World Traveler

NorDrey Books: Missoula, Montana
Nonfiction, fiction, audiobooks, and fine art photography

WEBSITE
www.NorDreyBooks.com

ESSAYS
www.RichardSpeights.com

BOOKS AVAILABLE ON AMAZON.COM
Paperback and Ebook and KDP Select

NORDREY BOOKS

Burnt Pancakes and Crummy Biscuits
The Cookbook
Patricia Ann Herren
(Available only in paper back, but also available at BarneAndNoble.com)

Where A Wild Wind Blows
Short Story Collection
Boyd Wolf

IN THE WORKS

Propaganda, Illusion of Guilt,
and the Value of Innocence
M. Richard Speights

The Day The Elephants Forgot Themselves
Sir Pipkin Longshanks

Lying Spirit

What Man Sees
Versus
What God Says

First Edition
M. Richard Speights

NorDrey Books
Missoula, Montana

Contents

	Introduction - God Does Not Lie	17
1	Mistranslation	25
2	Words	39
3	Lying Spirit Host of Heaven	53
4	The Prevailing View	77
5	The Two Previous Battles	85
6	Chess and the Battlefield Formation	105
7	Breakdown Of Events 1 Kings 22:1-28	143
8	The Battle 1 Kings 22:29-36	165
9	GN-z11	183

New King James

This book references mainly the New King James Version. This is done, not due to the accuracy of the version, but for expediency. The NKJV, like all English translations, has numerous faults, flaws, and translation errors. Occasionally, this work will make noted reference to other versions, such as the King James Version, the Concordant Literal Translation, Young's Literal Version, and others. This author utilizes Biblegateway.com, the Interlinear Scripture Analyzer 3, Strong's Greek and Hebrew lexicons through Studybible.info, and numerous other resources.

God cannot lie.

Titus 1:2

INTRODUCTION

GOD DOES NOT LIE

In 1 Kings 22 and 2 Chronicles 18, the prophet Micaiah revealed a vision. In this vision, God sends a lying spirit into the mouths of the four hundred paganized Jewish prophets. Now, this seems an odd event, for a number of verses say God does not lie. If so, then he would not cause a lie by proxy.

For example, in Balaam's blessing on God's people, he said:

> " 'God is not a man, that he should lie, nor a son of man, that he should repent. Has he said, and

will he not do? Or has he spoken, and will he not make it good?' " (Numbers 23:19)

And the Apostle Paul wrote:

> "Paul, a bondservant of God and an apostle of Jesus Christ, according to the faith of God's elect and the acknowledgment of the truth which accords with godliness, in hope of eternal life which **God, who cannot lie,** promised before time began, but has in due time manifested His word through preaching, which was committed to me according to the commandment of God our Savior…" (Titus 1:1-3, Emphasis mine)

Again, Paul wrote:

> "…Indeed, let God be true but every man a liar. As it is written: "That you [God] may be justified in your words, and may overcome when you are judged." (Romans 3:4)

These verses do seem at odds with Micaiah's vision. Moreover, Paul wrote in his second letter from Paul, Silvanus, and Timothy to the Thessalonians:

> "The coming of the lawless one is according to the working of Satan, with all power, signs, and lying wonders, and with all unrighteous deception among those who perish, because they did not receive the love of the truth, that they might be saved. And **for this reason God will send them strong delusion**, that they should believe the lie, that they all may be condemned who did not believe the truth but had pleasure in unrighteousness." (2 Thessalonians 2:9-12, Emphasis mine)

Of course, debate rages over the identity of the lawless one. Nonetheless, the idea God would send the lover of a lie strong delusion is, like Micaiah's vision, contrary to Paul and Balaam's declarations concerning God's incapacity to lie.

Above all else, freewill, which God gave man, demands God stay out of his creation's individual decision-making process. God calls us to obedience only. He does not compel obedience to his plan of salvation but promises to reward the faithful and punish the unwilling. He does not make a person do good or evil. So, through freewill, we do what we do and are fully capable of deluding ourselves.

So, why did Paul say God would send the lovers of lies strong delusions?

The language in Micaiah's vision is the same language Moses used when he wrote God hardened Pharaoh's heart. God did not actually harden Pharaoh's heart. Pharaoh's heart was primed for hardness from the beginning. Since God had the ability to put it in Pharaoh's mind to let the Jews go and, due to freewill, did not , then God, in a way, hardened the Egyptian monarch's heart. The language is a form of hyperbole, an exaggerated claim of action that never actually took place.

> Then again, he did trick the Syrians into believing a massive army was coming, causing them to abandon all their possessions as they fled in terror (2 Kings 7:6, 7). He also caused the Syrian charioteers to recognize Jehoshaphat to desist their attack (2 Chronicles 18:31, 32). There is an answer to the difference, which the book covers further in chapter eight.

Not only is God incapable of lying, he won't cause someone to lie or cause a lie through an agent. If so, then what of Micaiah's assertion he sent a lying spirit into the mouths of the prophets?

The answer to this particular dilemma lies in translational error. God did not send an actual spiritual being from the spiritual realm to make the prophets lie. Micaiah's vision is an allegory. The mistranslation, however, perverted this perfectly good metaphoric story into an odd literal event. As an allegory, the message is sublime. As a literal event, the message is an idiotic distortion of reality.

Regarding lying and causing a lie: The mistranslation in this case was purposeful, a product of Catholic interference with and influence on all English translations. The irony of purposefully influencing a mistranslation, which falsely makes God appear to cause a lie, is rich but not surprising. Jesus said wolves in sheep's clothing would ravage the flock. Paul said men would pervert the word of truth. John said liars were already among God's people at the writing of his letters and would remain.

Mistranslations abound in all English versions of the Bible. This book, Lying Spirit, focuses on the flaws contained in the English translations of 1 Kings 22 and its companion, 2 Chronicles 18. Beyond the misrepresentation of Micaiah's vision, the report on the events surrounding the vision says one thing but the religious world sees it as another. It's time to correct this misunderstanding too.

Let us then apply ourselves to Paul's admonition: "Be diligent to present yourself approved to God, a worker who does not need to be ashamed, rightly dividing the word of truth." (2 Timothy 2:15)

Never trust the translation or interpretation of something without first trusting its interpreter. One word absent from a sentence can drastically change the true intended meaning of the entire sentence. For instance, if the word 'love' is intentionally or accidentally replaced with 'hate' in a sentence, its effect could trigger a war or false dogma.

Suzy Kassem

ONE

MISTRANSLATION

There are many commentaries claiming to explain the so-called lying spirit.

This is not one of them.

Commentators tend to write in the subjective, offering opinions instead of studied explanations. Giving one's impression of biblical passages or guessing their meanings is not the same as deciphering meaning through an objective approach.

Secondly, something is wrong with the religious world's handling of 1 Kings 22 and 2 Chronicles 18. While the explanations for the lying spirit diverge dramatically between commentators, which are expected, the uniform explanation of the events surrounding Micaiah's vision is out of character.

This single explanation is truly odd, for the religious world rarely agrees on any subject. It is as if someone in the past wrote a paper on the events in 1 Kings 22, and everyone simply adopted his theses wholesale.

This book disagrees with all the explanations for the so-called lying spirit as it disagrees with the one explanation given for the events leading up to the battle for Ramoth-Gilead and the battle itself.

Nonetheless, this work is not the product of opinion. The author does not base his exposition on subjective reasoning. This work is not an intellectual pontification. The author approaches the subjects objectively. He does not guess. He does not presume. He does not dream up explanations from the resources of his own mind. He presents the facts according to known realities, and the facts reveal the truth concerning both Micaiah's vision and the events surrounding the Jewish kings' battle against Benhadad for Ramoth-Gilead.

Jesus called Satan the father of lies (John 8:44). The devil is a true master of deception. In this, he tells his most convincing lies by influencing men to twist God's words in the guise of the grand search for truth. A number of motivations drive them. But, whatever the incentive, replacing biblical works with one's own puts words in God's mouth.

Truly, where is the finite man able to do such a thing?

While Satan had no influence on the prophets and other biblical writers, he exercised tremendous influence on the English translators. But, this is no surprise. He is cunning. By influencing the translators to alter the text, he presents lies as truth.

So, he subverts the translators, who then subvert the words, which then subvert the English-speaking world. Subverting the English-speaking world spawns doctrinal and intellectual chaos, sowing modern tares in this modern age. Very clever, for mistranslations and misrepresentations cause the biblical reader to think he has learned truth when he has actually adopted deceit.

The Apostle John touched on the difference between God's word and Satan's: "Then I saw another beast coming up out of the earth, and he had two horns like a lamb and spoke like a dragon." (Revelation 13:11)

In other words, the beast presents itself as Christ-like while twisting God's words into sermons of Satan.

These translational faults are not limited to the King James Version. All English translations of the Bible suffer errors. Some versions are shoddier than others. Paraphrased works, as a dramatic example, are the most egregious. They absolutely cannot claim accuracy. These versions of the Bible are a summarization of a translation of an ancient language. As a copy of a copy of the original, this type of work is the product of diminishing returns. Actually, it is worse, for a paraphrase version of the Bible is fiction masquerading as fact.

Beyond this, even translations claiming substantial accuracy suffer flaws. Some flaws are due to failure to fully understand the original text. Some are due to personal, arrogance-driven interpretation. Some are due to the translators' lack of knowledge in grammar. Some are due to doctrinal influence, goading the translators to reword the original to fit a particular religious belief, notion, or philosophy.

This lack of knowledge in the rules of grammar is particularly surprising, for one would assume translators should be steeped in the rules governing language. This problem is not limited to only a couple of biblical verses.

Sometimes, the translators, attempting to add literary value, simply ignored certain inconvenient grammatical rules. Paul's comment on money in his letter to Timothy stands as a prime example. Paul did not say the love of money is the root of all evil. He also did not say the love of money is the root of all kinds of evil. He said something else, but the translators were so enthusiastic to add literary value to his prose they destroyed the antecedent-proform relationship transforming Paul's intended meaning into a declaration of general truth.[1]

As originally written, the Bible is more instruction manual than literary masterpiece. The earliest translations, especially the King James, reworked the prose, transforming meaningful passages into literary gobbledygook. Certainly, passages rewritten to provide literary value beautifully roll off the tongue. However, rolling off the tongue was not necessarily God's intent.

Matthew 5:5 stands as a good example. The words in the English translation ring, but Jesus did not actually say the meek would inherit the Earth. He used similar words, but similarity is to accuracy as salt is to sugar. The English translation is worthless drivel. It sounds great, but it hides Jesus's intended meaning. When translators pervert biblical words, the reader loses the point.

And, from the very first English translation, doctrinal interference, specifically Catholicism, influenced the translators to purposefully manipulate the text. Matthew 5:5 stands as a good example, for the message Jesus actually gave does not align with Catholic doctrine. So, it is natural the Catholics influenced the early translators to fudge the language. Thereafter, everyone, including Young's Literal, followed suit. Catholic influence is as powerful as it is pervasive.

Catholic influenced mistranslation is much more prevalent than the common reader recognizes, and it affects all translations. Every Christian who immerses for salvation knows the Catholic Church influenced the translators to pervert the Greek word, *baptizo*, by coining a new word, *baptize*. There is only one reason to do so. They were hiding the truth to support a lie.

Yet, these non-Catholics immersers, while pointing an accusatory finger at the word, *baptize*, fail to realize the translators also coined a number of other important words. And through the years, these Catholic-influenced novel words, phrases, and passages have become part of the modern lexicon.

All translations repeat these new words, including, to a lesser degree, literal translations. The words Heaven, church, baptize, angel, and cross, for example, are words every Christian uses despite the fact they are Catholic inventions and nowhere found in the original text.

This is no small thing. "Great oaks from little acorns grow." A false notion derived from a single mistranslated word has the potential to develop into a worldwide, false religious belief system. It certainly sows intellectual disorder.

This book focuses upon 1 Kings 22, wherein we find a number of mistranslations. Two mistranslations specifically cause major problems for readers, influencing them, and every commentator on the planet, to believe God sent an actual spiritual being from the spiritual realm to cause Ahab's four hundred prophets to lie. This is not what the original prose claims. Jeremiah wrote no such thing. No spiritual being entered the mouths of the Jewish-pagan prophets. God did not send anyone to do anything.

Micaiah's vision is figurative. The prophet gave his vision in the form of an allegorical. Reading the words as originally written, and recognizing word usage of that time, the allegorical nature of the prose is perfectly clear. Yet, from the earliest English translation, the mishandled language has destroyed the metaphor, transforming the symbolic imagery into a literal event.

This isn't the only problem. In 1 Kings 22, Jeremiah provided information about the events surrounding the vision in snippets. The prose hits the highlights without much explanation. Due to this sparseness, and a general lack of knowledge concerning military operations, the religious world has developed an erroneous view on what actually occurred in Samaria as the two Jewish kings prepared for battle and the battle itself.

All these things create an interesting peculiarity. The religious world is horribly divided, with thousands upon thousands of divergent expressions and beliefs. Yet, in atypical unity, it holds a singular explanation for the events involving the preparation for battle and the battle. Except for minor differences, the religious world has adopted a single view. This is truly bizarre.

Nonetheless, unity of thought does not always equate to rightness, a maxim especially true in this case. The current unified view does not recognize the Jewish kings' brilliant plan to split the Syrian army in two and surround each half with an independent army, two armies led, of course, by two Jewish kings. Ahab did not have Jehoshaphat take his place out of fear, Zechariah's iron horns did not represent the two kings, Jehoshaphat did not cry out in fear, and Micaiah spoke not in mocking tones. Overall, the errant explanation is born of the imagination and not the product of dedicated research and factual knowledge.

I can't think of another issue like this. It makes sense every commentator diverges in his explanation of the lying spirit. People certainly feel free to speculate answers to symbolic and metaphoric language, and speculation always creates a plethora of divergent explanations. Still, that such a divided people have reached such a singular explanation for the events in 1 Kings 22 is a unique occurrence.

Three Parts

The twenty-second chapter in 1 Kings and its companion, 2 Chronicles 18, records the event in three parts, the preparation for the battle, Micaiah's vision, and the battle for Ramoth-Gilead.

The vision aside, the prose describing these events is not complicated. However, as it provides information in bits and pieces it paints a picture with a broad brush. The sparseness of these meager details has clearly mystified both readers and commentators. Nonetheless, there is enough information to determine exactly what the two Jewish kings did and why they did it.

At the risk of repeating myself, guessing meaning is an ongoing problem in the religious world. When facing passages of obscure meaning, readers are too often tempted to speculate answers. However, speculation does not accurately decipher passages, difficult or easy. Speculation is another word for guessing, and a guess is to accuracy as sightlessness is to threading a needle.

For example, imagine two men find a water well long abandoned. Peering down into the dark hole, they both guess its depth. Now, while only one of these two guesses can be correct, they are both likely wrong. Until the men measure the depth with a standard, their guesses do not carry the weight of truth, for unverified speculation has no legitimate claim to it.

Einstein's theory of general relativity is a good real world example. Oh, boy, but how his paper set physicists atwitter. Nonetheless, the science community could not declare his theory substantially accurate until Sir Arthur Eddington photographed a solar eclipse, proving a key claim in the thesis: Gravity affects light.[2]

Posing a hypothesis is an acceptable beginning point, but the researcher must not treat a thesis as the end product of intellectual pursuit. Truth's discovery demands putting knowledge to the test. When a belief, theory, or speculation survives scrutiny, then good. When they fail, then also good – for knowing what is wrong is as important as knowing what is right. What did Edison say? "I have not failed. I've just found 10,000 ways that won't work."

So, the religious world's view on Micaiah's vision is off base due to mistranslation and misrepresentation. Meanwhile, the errant view on the preparation for the battle and the battle itself is due to people speculating answers without sufficient knowledge and scrutiny.

When one reads, he or she must do so with an open mind. It is good to ask oneself if there is an answer or explanation better than the one currently held. The biblical student must never be satisfied but check and double check to make certain he is accurate in all things.

Of course, always remember to ask God for wisdom (James 1:5).

Now, more often than not, the biblical text is self-explanatory. Sometimes, information from different passages combine for a better understanding of their meaning. However, in 1 Kings 22, to understand what these two Jewish kings did depends upon possession of information found in a source outside the biblical text.

Nonetheless, this information is not mysterious or difficult to find. Specifically, the reader needs a basic knowledge of battlefield formations, tactics, and strategies. It also helps to be familiar with the tricks armies play and have played on enemies throughout history to gain strategic or tactical advantage.

In the following chapters, let's find the flaws and correct the mistranslated passages. Thereafter, let's fill in the informational gaps for a better understanding of Jeremiah's historical record.

Footnotes:

1	1 Timothy 6:9, 10

2	Sir Author Eddington
	https://en.wikipedia.org/wiki/Arthur_Eddington
	[Relativity]

In the beginning was the word...

                                                              John 1:1

TWO

WORDS

The Bible is a collection of words. Reading the words as originally written reveals God's message. Replacement words interjected into the script muddle his intended meaning.

The Catholics dominated the world for many hundreds of years. In this time, they influenced the world's ideas on religion, Jesus, God's message, and his plan of salvation. They also influenced the mistranslations found in every version we read. Moreover, many of their purposeful misrepresented words have found their way into language and common usage.

Common usage does not necessarily equate with correctness. The biblical student must not automatically accept a word as true and correct, simply because everyone on the planet uses it. This is evident in the previous example, *baptize* instead of *immerse*. The first word hides the truth. The latter is the truth. The soul looking for truth would do well to abandon the fabricated, find the original, and stick to it.

To understand an author's intended meaning, a person must read the words the author actually wrote. Translators undermine original meaning when they replace the original words with novel words and word phrases. A mistranslated word creates a dishonest work.

The gold miner does not reach the precious yellow metal through casual efforts. Likewise, the dedicated biblical student will not find truth through half measures. The dedicated put words to the test.

To accept translated words unquestioned is like following hand painted road signs. They may lead to the desired destination. Chances are, they do not. The traveler cannot be certain until it is too late. Discovering the truth on Judgment Day is one day too late.

A word may ring true, but the world is full of illusions. Like the Louisiana truck driver who mistakenly hauled his load all the way to Jacksonville, Florida, instead of Jackson, Mississippi, sounding right is not the same as being right.

Verification also goes for commentaries and other materials, religious and secular. The one in search of truth must not automatically accept everything people write as accurate. Throughout history, people have penned far more false words than true. Writers are human and prone to error.

The Holy Spirit did not and does not guide the translator's hands. Something about the work seems to promote arrogance. From the beginning, hubris has driven translators to interpret rather than translate.

In 1 Kings 22, English translators all the way back to Wycliffe have mishandled Micaiah's vision by mistranslating two key word phrases. They mistranslated the first word phrase due to Catholic influence. They misrepresented the second by interpreting rather than translating, inspired by the first mistranslated word no doubt.

Young's Literal Translation does a good job translating the two particular phrases in question. Unfortunately, most people do not reference Young's. People become generally enamored with whatever version they use, and the emotional connection influences them to accept what they read as error free.

People simply do not ordinarily think to double-check the translators' work. Also, when a person learns of a particular error, it does not usually occur to make corrections on the printed page. The words, "Holy Bible," may grace the cover, but the physical book is not a holy relic.

It is reasonable and right for a reader to scratch through a mistranslated word, phrase, or passage and write the accurate word or words in the margin – always, of course, double and triple checking for accuracy.

This is imperative. As a ship will not reach its destination with a defective compass, a person cannot discover God's will through an instruction manual full of altered prose. Micaiah's vision stands as a grand example. Although his message is sublime, it took only two seemingly insignificant errors to transform a wonderfully crafted allegory into an absurd, oddly worded literal event.

Two Mistranslated Word Phrases

The two word phrases in question are *host of Heaven* and *lying spirit*, *tzba eshmim* and *ruch shqr* respectively. First, the translators mistranslated the original word phrase, *hosts of the heavens*. Then, they either misunderstood the original, *spirit of falsehood*, due to the previous mistranslation or they simply misrepresented when adding literary value.

So, the problem started with a mistranslation, which muddled the meaning. This then led to a misrepresentation, due to the previous mistranslation. This is the nature of the beast, a slippery slope of error, created by interpretation instead of faithful translation. Nonetheless, once clarified, the meaning of the vision becomes apparent.

Host / Hosts

A word spelled the same with different meanings is a homograph. For example: Does a bear care about the burden you bear?

The word *host* in Hebrew, *tzba*, acts as a type of homograph. The core meaning is a gathered group or a gathering of groups. So, while the Hebrew writers sometimes used it to mean tribe, they also used the word to mean an army.

Moses used the Hebrew word, *tzbauthikm*, in Exodus, referencing the twelve tribes of Israel leaving Egypt. The word accurately translates into English as *hosts of you*.

> " '…and ye have observed the unleavened things, for in this self-same day I have brought out **your hosts** from the land of Egypt…' " (Exodus 12:17, Young's Literal Translation, bold mine (more accurately, hosts of you))

By using the word *hosts of you* (note the plural), Moses meant God had brought the Jewish tribes and subdivisions of tribes out of the land of Egypt. However, the King James translators often turned to the Septuagint when translating the Old Testament. The Jews in Alexander translated the Hebrew and Aramaic into Greek about 200 BC. Again, like the paraphrased translations, a translation of a translation is a copy of a copy. So, a translation of a translation simply exacerbates whatever mistranslations the Septuagint translators previously created.

When the Jewish translators reached Exodus 12:17 in the Septuagint, they translated the Hebrew word, *tzbauthikm (hosts of you)*, into the Greek word, *daimonia* (δύναμις or δυναμεις). This Greek word translates into English as *force*, as in; the Jews came out of Egypt with their forces. The King James boys then interpreted the mistranslated Greek word, *daimonia* (force), and translated it as *armies*.

So, the Hebrew word, *tzbauthikm*, goes from *hosts of you* to *force* to *armies*, another example of the literary slippery slope.

I do not know why they did this. The mistranslation is rather absurd. As slaves in Egypt, the Jews did not possess armies. They were not a force. They had no power. God specifically sent Moses to relieve them of their bondage through the Lord's own power. The Jews were helpless in Egypt just as they were helpless at the Red Sea, vulnerable and panicked by the approaching Egyptian army. This errant word choice skews meaning, implying power where no power existed. The translators should have not interpreted but translated words as written. This and many other errors show they were not truly interested in accuracy in significant and insignificant passages alike.

As for its use in 1 Kings 22, *tzba* (hosts) has a third usage. The Hebrew word also means a group of objects or groups of objects. In this case, the word phrase, *hosts of the heavens*, means the stars in the sky.

Spirit

As the Hebrew word for *host* has more than one meaning, the word for *spirit, ruch,* also has more than one[1]. Mostly, as people know, it means a spiritual being from the spiritual realm, such as *uruch aleim*, spirit of Elohim (Spirit of God).

However, it can also mean the nature of a thing, such as:

> "For the Lord has poured out on you the spirit of deep sleep [*ruch thrdme*], and has closed your eyes, namely, the prophets; and he has covered your heads, namely, the seers." (Isaiah 29:10).

The following is but a limited sampling of the word phrase, *spirit of,* used to mean the nature of a thing:

- Spirit of wisdom, Deuteronomy 34:9
- Spirit of jealousy, Numbers 5:30
- Spirit of heaviness, Isaiah 61:3
- Spirit of harlotry, Hosea 5:4
- Spirit of grace and supplication, Zechariah 12:10
- Spirit of truth, John 16:13
- Spirit of holiness, Romans 1:4
- Spirit of prophecy, Revelation 19:10
(NKJV)

Heaven / Heavens

The word, *Heaven*, meaning the place of God's abode, is ubiquitous, used everywhere by everyone in both the religious world and secular. However, this word as a proper noun is nowhere found in the original Hebrew, Aramaic, or Greek. The biblical text simply does not name God's abode.

The word in all three ancient languages is plural, *heavens*, a common noun. As a proper noun, it is supposed to be capitalized. Notice, however, how translations rarely capitalized it. This is creative spelling, using the word as a proper noun but spelled it as a common noun. After all, the translators know (or are supposed to know) the original text did not actually name God's spiritual realm. The Hebrew word is simply *eshmim*, the heavens (Also *shmim*, which is still plural. The difference between the two Hebrew words, *eshmim* and *shmim*, is the difference between *in the heavens* and *the heavens*).

Yes, Paul in Corinthians[2] wrote about a fellow who went to the third heaven. Since the daytime sky is the first heaven and the nighttime sky is the second, then the place beyond the visible would be the third. Nonetheless, Paul wrote third heaven as a common noun and not as a proper noun. His calling it *the third heaven*, (more accurately, *the third heavens*), does not automatically transform the word *heavens* into *Heaven*.

This is not a matter of semantics. A misrepresented word skews meaning. Skewing meaning causes confusion. Catholicism is the source of these mistranslated words, in which they reshape the biblical text to make scripture fit their perverted doctrine.

This makes sense when we recognize Catholicism for what it is, an ancient pagan religion disguised in the robes of Christianity. Once acknowledged, their odd beliefs, behaviors, rituals, ceremonies, practices, icons, imageries, and religious protocols began to make sense. They pervert everything holy into pagan practices, transforming Godly worship into ancient, worldly expressions. Meaningless gestures are the hallmark of paganism, and Catholicism, along with her twin sister, Greek Orthodox, and her illegitimate child, Anglicanism, are replete with them.

From 1534 AD to publication of the King James Bible, there wasn't a spit of difference between Catholicism and the Church of England. Beyond the politics, to say Catholicism was to say Anglican. Although the translators worked under the head of the Church of England, Catholic doctrine was still the driving force behind the purposeful misrepresentations.

They perverted words and coined new ones. Since paganism loves mysteries and mysticisms, it is natural they transformed *heavens* into *Heaven*, for this perversion transforms God into a mysterious creature, living in a mystical place.

The Catholics dominated the world for hundreds of years. That was a long time to indoctrinate Western societies into these perverted paganistic notions, beliefs, and imageries. This long-term influence shaped how the world viewed God. The biblical reader who wants the truth must avoid their influence. The honest Christian chooses not to use unique words of human origin. The faithful biblical student sticks only with the words God provided.

God's words contain life. Man's words produce spiritual death. These creators of novel words are the wolves in sheep's clothing Jesus mentioned, speaking lies to institutionalize evil, soul killing practices.

Footnotes:

1. Strong's Hebrew Lexicon
   https://studybible.info/strongs/H7307
   Strong's lexicons and dictionaries have some deficits. For a couple of examples, they insist on defining *stauron* as *cross* and *baptizo* as *baptize*, keying on common usage instead of accuracy. They also fail to recognize the nuance usage of the word, *ruch*, as the nature of a thing. Strong's sometimes appears more interested in appeasing religious entities, specifically Catholicism, than remaining true to the word. If they did it right, they would ignore common usage altogether.

2. 2 Corinthians 12:2
   "I know a man in Christ who fourteen years ago – whether in the body I do not know, or whether out of the body I do not know, God knows – such a one was caught up to the third heaven." (NKJV)

Translation is that which transforms everything so that nothing changes.

> Günter Grass

THREE

LYING SPIRIT
HOST OF HEAVEN

The replacement of true words with false has caused a world of trouble for people attempting to understand Micaiah's vision. To know what the writer meant, we must read the words he wrote and not the words someone devised he wrote.

Host of the Heavens / Hosts of the Heavens

The translator's mishandling of the word phrase in 1 Kings 22 made the passage's true meaning impossible to discern. All translations except Young's mistranslate the Hebrew word phrase, *tzba eshmim*, in 1 Kings 22:19.

Instead of translating it correctly as *hosts of the heavens*, they translate it as *host of Heaven*.

New King James Version

> "Then Micaiah said, 'Therefore hear the word of the Lord: I saw the Lord sitting on His throne, and all the **host of heaven** standing by, on His right hand and on His left'. " (Bold mine (Note the word *heaven* is singular and not plural.)

Young's Literal Translation

> "And he saith, 'Therefore, hear a word of Jehovah; I have seen Jehovah sitting on His throne, and all the **host of the heavens** standing by Him, on His right and on His left…' " (Bold mine (hosts of the heavens))

The mistranslated word phrase causes everyone to incorrectly connect Micaiah's vision with the first chapter of Job:

> "Now there was a day when the sons of God came to present themselves before the Lord, and Satan also came among them." (Job 1:6)

While *host of heaven* sounds like a gathering of spiritual beings, the original phrase, *hosts of the heavens*, has nothing to do with the spiritual realm. This word phrase, used repeatedly throughout scripture, refers to the field of visible stars in the night sky, the hosts of stars or host of stars.

> (Young's wrote *host* in the singular. The original word in Hebrew is *hosts*, a plural. This refers to the gathered groups of stars, i.e., the constellations.)

Including its usage in Kings and Chronicles, the biblical writers employed this word phrase nineteen times in scripture.

Four times, the word phrase simply references the stars:

- Nehemiah 9:6
- Isaiah 34:4
- Jeremiah 33:22
- Daniel 8:10

However, fifteen times the word phrase references the stars in connection to pagan worship, astrology/zodiac:

- Deuteronomy 4:19
- Deuteronomy 17:3
- 1 Kings 22:19
- 2 Kings 17:16
- 2 Kings 21:3
- 2 Kings 21:5
- 2 Kings 23:4
- 2 Kings 23:5
- 2 Chronicles 18:18
- 2 Chronicles 33:3
- 2 Chronicles 33:5
- Jeremiah 8:2
- Jeremiah 19:13
- Zephaniah 1:5
- Acts 7:42

Notice how the mistranslated word phrase in Deuteronomy makes no sense as written in English: " 'And take heed, lest you lift your eyes to heaven, and when you see the sun, the moon, and the stars, all the **host of heaven**, you feel driven to worship them and serve them, which the Lord your God has given to all the peoples under the whole heaven as a heritage'. " (Deuteronomy 4:19 NKJV)

Of course, the above should read, *hosts of the heavens*. As written, the misguided phrase, *host of heaven*, seems to include the spiritual realm with physical astrological bodies. Do note: The original script says, "and the stars, and the hosts of the heavens," distinguishing between the two.

Let me paraphrase for clarity. "…least you lift your eyes to the heavens, to the Sun, Moon, stars, and constellations and feel compelled to worship them."

Note: The phrase, *hosts of the heavens*, refers to constellations, because the zodiac, through which the pagans worship the stars, is based on the constellations and not necessarily upon individual stars.

So, if the word phrase, *hosts of the heavens*, means the constellations, then Micaiah's vision has God's throne sitting not in the spiritual realm but positioned among the stars. This makes his vision an allegory and not a record of a literal event.

Now, as God allegorically sat on his throne among the stars, he asks which of the stars or constellations will persuade Ahab to go to Ramoth-Gilead. This triggered a debate among the twinkling lights until a spirit stepped forward with a solution.

Since a literal God is allegorically speaking to literal stars, and since literal stars do not have literal spirits, then the spirit coming before God in 1 Kings 22's is figurative. God did not send a literal spiritual being, either a messenger or demon, to possess the prophets. His allegory vision simply accuses the four hundred prophets of dishonesty in their worship of the stars and pretense of prophecy through the zodiac.

Moreover, these four hundred prophets did not need God to cause them to speak falsely. They were already steeped in the spirit of falsehood through their pagan worship. Micaiah's vision is simply shining a bright allegorical light on this behavior, even when he spoke in declaratory terms:

> " 'And now, lo, Jehovah hath put a spirit of falsehood in the mouth of all these thy prophets, and Jehovah hath spoken concerning thee – evil'. " (1 Kings 22:23 YLT)

If Micaiah were reporting literal things, then the language would certainly claim God caused the pagan prophets to speak falsehoods. The figurative nature of the language dampens this assumption. Additionally, Moses employed similar language in Exodus concerning

Pharaoh. "But the Lord hardened the heart of Pharaoh…" (Exodus 9:12)

This declaratory language, used a few times in the Bible, throws some people. Why, they ask, would God harden the Egyptian leader's heart and put a spirit of falsehood into the prophets' mouths? After all, Pharaoh and the four hundred prophets were freewill agents. Does God interfere with freewill choice?

The answer is, no. God does not interfere. Still, in a way, he did harden Pharaoh's heart and put false words in the prophet's mouths.

Think of it this way. There's a farmer. He's upset his upstream neighbor has dammed the creek. So, he places dynamite against the blockage and pours out a line of gunpowder as a fuse. The farmer lights this gunpowder and plugs his ears for the coming kaboom. Meanwhile, a man with a bucket of water stands beside the line of gunpowder, halfway between the dam and the farmer. Bucket man can easily stop the advancing flaming fuse with a quick douse.

However, he does not.

Since bucket man has the power to stop the explosion and does not, then he, in a way, also destroys the dam. This is the logic behind the language declaring God hardened Pharaoh's heart and put a spirit of falsehood in the mouths of the prophets.

God could have easily put it in Pharaoh's mind to let the Jews go. He could have just as easily put it in the minds of the four hundred prophets to warn Ahab to stay home. He could have caused the two kings to refrain. However, doing so would have robbed all these people their freewill choices. Good or evil, a man must choose his path and then live his choice. God does not subvert the choices of his creation.

Micaiah's vision placing God's throne among the constellations reveals the four hundred prophets were utilizing the zodiac to advise their king. Nonetheless, there was more to the four hundred Jewish-pagan prophet's fortune-telling ability than simply consulting the stars. Since the stars are quite unable to predict future events, then the four hundred were also using other means to make accurate or semi-accurate predictions. The vision simply points out their worship of the stars as the focal point of their falseness.

Overall, the allegory highlights the contrast between human rebellion and obedience. The four hundred prophets did not consult God but consulted the stars. Micaiah did not consult the stars; he consulted God. Ahab's prophets, basing their prophecy on the zodiac and the things they could see with their own eyes, gave a falsely inspired report in the pretense of God's truth. Micaiah did not turn to paganism or allow his eyes to fool him but delivered a true report by speaking only the words God provided.

Now, consider Jehoshaphat's behavior: He may have asked for a word from the Lord, but he disregarded God's word and believed his own eyes and the four hundred Jewish-pagan prophets. This shows he wasn't looking for God's input as much as he was looking only for a good word.

Important Note: The positive word from these four hundred prophets was not the only convincer. Everything the prophets saw told them the two Jewish kings would win the battle. Everything the two kings saw told them the same. Victory filled their eyes, blinding them to God's word of defeat.

This freewill thing is an important running theme

throughout the Bible. Freewill allows choice. However, to choose, one must have a choice. Adam and Eve had the tree of knowledge in the Garden. God did not plant it on top of the highest mountain. He did not set it on another continent. He made it super easy to reach. The tree was in the midst of the garden with low hanging fruit. "So when the woman saw that the tree was good for food, that it was pleasant to the eyes, and a tree desirable to make one wise, she took of its fruit and ate."[1] To facilitate freewill, the tree was just a short stroll away, its fruit within easy reach.

As Adam and Eve had a choice to obey God or not, the two kings, sitting on their thrones in their kingly robes, chose to ignore God and hear the voice of the prophets, who spoke, not according to God, but in the spirit of falsehood.

Lying Spirit / Spirit of Falsehood

The word, *lying*, is a present participle of the verb *lie*. It modifies the noun, *spirit*, implying action. Therefore, a lying spirit is a spirit who lies.

On the other hand, the word, *falsehood*, is a noun, descriptive and passive. The word phrase, *spirit of falsehood*, does not depict an active spiritual being but characterizes the nature of falseness.

The NKJV, like all other versions of the Bible except the Young's, mistranslates the word:

> " 'The Lord said to him, "In what way?" So he said, "I will go out and be a **lying spirit** in the mouth of all his prophets". ' " (1 Kings 22:22 NKJV, bold mine)

However the original script, literally translated, reads as:

> "and he saith, I go out, and have been a **spirit of falsehood** in the mouth of all his prophets; and He saith, Thou dost entice, and also thou art able; go out and do so." (1 Kings 22:22 Young's Literal Translation, bold mine)[2]

When the translators used the term, lying spirit, they interpreted instead of translated. This interjected their own beliefs and ideas instead of transcribing the words as originally written. They came to their erroneous idea by first mistranslating the word phrase, host of the heavens. Then, believing God was in the spiritual realm, they concluded he sent an actual spiritual messenger or demon to cause Ahab's prophets to lie. One wrong led to another.

This impulse is so strong, even the Concordant Literal Version fudged the words, translating the word phrase as *false spirit* instead of *spirit of falsehood*. The word, *false*, now acts to modify the word, *spirit*, which implies a spiritual being speaking falsely. This is just as wrong as the word phrase *lying spirit*.

Young's Literal Translation is apparently the only version to translate the word phrase correctly from the Hebrew: ruch=spirit / shqr=falsehood.

It is clear the translators did not consider biblical usage. That is, they did not account for the word phrase's use elsewhere in the Bible, our best source for defining meaning. Nonetheless, the biblical writers used this phrase, *spirit of*, throughout the Bible to mean the nature of a thing. For example:

> "…when the **spirit of jealousy** [*ruch qnae*] comes upon a man, and he becomes jealous of his wife; then he shall stand the woman before the Lord…" (Numbers 5:30, bold mine).

The following are additional examples of the word phrase, *spirit of,* used in the Bible:

- Isaiah 4:4 *ruch mshpht,* spirit of judgment
- Isaiah 4:4 *ruch bor,* spirit of burning or consuming
- Isaiah 28:6 *ruch emshpht,* spirit of judgment or justice
- Isaiah 29:10 *ruch thrdme,* spirit of deep sleep (stupor)
- Hosea 4:12 *ruch znunim,* spirit of harlotry

The New Testament writers also used this phrase in Greek:

- Romans 8:15 *pneuma huiothesias,* spirit of adoption
- Romans 11:8 *pneuma katanuxeOs,* spirit of stupor (deep sleep)
- 1 Corinthians 4:21 *pneuma prautEtos,* spirit of gentleness (meekness)[3]

Additionally, and significant to the allegory in 1 Kings 22, while all lies are falsehoods, not all falsehoods are lies. This may seem oxymoronic, but a man can speak a falsehood truthfully. For example, a man in 1000 AD might teach his children the Sun orbits the Earth. He would not be lying. He would be as wrong as Pico de

Gallo on a banana split, but based upon everything he knew through the science of his day, he would be speaking what he believed to be the truth.

Although Ahab's pagan prophets operated under a spirit of falsehood, they would not have sent their king to his doom by knowingly lying to him. They actually believed the words they spoke, based both upon their reading of the zodiac and the intelligence they gathered through observations. In other words, they believed what they saw over what God had said.

One Thing Leads To Another

Two mistranslations in 1 Kings 22 led to a complete misunderstanding of Micaiah's vision. This is a perfect example of how a few mistranslated words can alter meaning. The Catholic Church started by inspiring the mistranslation of *heavens* into *Heaven*. This mistranslation muddled Micaiah's vision, creating an illusion God was sitting on his throne in the spiritual realm.

Then, when the translators read verse twenty-one, " '…a spirit came forward and stood before the Lord', " they naturally concluded it was a literal spirit from the spiritual plane. So, motivated by this assumption, they reshaped the Hebrew phrase, *ruch shqr*, into *lying spirit* instead of *spirit of falsehood*.

This behavior is a prime example of men's preconception overruling actuality.

Ironically, the translators, by altering the text to befit Catholic doctrine, acted through the spirit of falsehood by replacing God's word with their own. This makes these passages reporting Micaiah's vision one of the most poignant ironies in all the misguided English translations.

Consider this: How many other misunderstandings did the Catholics create through the mischief of their hubris? The number of misunderstood passages is rather surprising, causing mass confusion and even spawning false doctrines. If, for example, the King James Bible were a college textbook, professors would reject it, as containing too many flaws.

The Allegory

Biblical prophecies are typically revealed metaphorically or symbolically. A metaphor renames a thing by reflection. For example, to say, "That man is a mountain," is renaming the big, strong man as something he reflects, a mountain.

An allegory takes this reflective nature and extends it in story form, a sustained metaphor. Now, this allegorical story says one thing but means another. The meaning is reflective, so it is easy to recognize. Symbolic language, on the other hand, says one thing and means another; but, the thing said does not reflect the thing meant. This language is in John's Book of Revelation, which makes the book terribly difficult to decipher. The meaning of Micaiah's vision, on the other hand, is easy to recognize.

George Orwell's book, Animal Farm, is a good example of an allegory. This book focused on the evils of communism. According to the study guide, sparknotes:

> "Animal Farm symbolizes Russia and the Soviet Union under Communist Party rule. The book portrays the internal structure of a nation, wherein the pigs represent the government, the dogs represent the police force or army, and the other animals represent the working class." (Edited)[4]

Likewise, Micaiah's vision is allegorical, a figurative story of reflection. In this allegory, God's throne sits among the stars. Then, through personification[5], a metaphor, God asks the stars a question, which triggers a debate.

Importantly, Micaiah's vision verifies Ahab's prophets worshiped and utilized the zodiac. Micaiah was painting a metaphoric picture of God quizzing to the very stars the Jewish-pagan prophets claim to consult. "Which one of you guys is going to persuade Ahab?"

In an episode of the long-running television series, The Naked Archeologist, Simcha Jacobovici investigated an archeological find beside the Sea of Galilee. This structure appears to have been a synagogue in the ancient past. However, the discovery was rather shocking, for a mosaic of the zodiac covered the structure's floor. After the episode aired, Mr. Jacobovici wrote a paper, clarifying his position on the building and its mosaic. In short, he simply could not believe a Jews would build a mosaic of a zodiac in a synagogue. He wrote, "Pagans didn't mind using Jewish symbols, or any other symbols for that matter. Jews, however, went to their death rather than allowing pagan symbols in their houses of worship'."[6]

Simcha may be a little off base in his assumption. The

Old Testament reveals the Jews in the Northern Kingdom adopted Baal, Asherah, and various other pagan gods for many years until their dissolution as a nation. This included worship of the zodiac. The people in the Southern Kingdom, Judah, dabbled in the same from time to time, but after seventy years captivity, they learned their lesson, calmed down, and stopped whoring with the occult.

Nonetheless, Simcha is giving his post-Babylonian ancestors a little too much credit. Sin is seductive. It should be no surprise some Jews in a later century would revert to pagan practices. Look at how the modern world is currently adopting all sorts of ancient paganism. They're not even hiding their behaviors but openly professing pagan beliefs. Yes, indeed; we've come back to the idiocy we once departed.

Zechariah, one of these four hundred prophets, did mix Judaism with paganism by the words, "Thus says the Lord." (1 Kings 22: 11) Clearly, the Jewish-pagan prophets mixed their worship of the zodiac with Godly religion in 850 BC. It follows some would do it again post Jerusalem's destruction. Moreover, it appears several ancient synagogues sported zodiac floors.

Conclusion

The vision is allegorical. It is not a record of real events occurring in the spiritual world. The *hosts of the heavens* are the constellations the four hundred prophets consulted before giving their advice. God, allegorically sitting among the stars, ironically asks them who will persuade Ahab. An allegorical spirit says it will be a nature of falsehood in the mouths of the pagan prophets.

Nonetheless, there is more to the story.

In the movie, *Willow*, the villagers do not know what to do with the Daikini baby the protagonist had earlier plucked from the river. So, the wizard announces, "I will consult the bones." He rattles the bits of bone in a gourd before tossing them on the ground. The old wizard and the young apprentice then bend over for a closer look. In this intimate moment, the old wizard confesses to his younger, "The bones tell me nothing." He then queries Willow for information. "Do you have any love for this child?" Only Willow's answer gives him the information he needs to make a decision. Notwithstanding, with a raised hand, the old wizard declares, "The bones have spoken."

Ahab's pagan prophets consulted the stars, but like the bones in Willow, the stars told them nothing. Claiming knowledge from the stars is the epitome of the spirit of falsehood. Like the wizard, they knew the truth – the zodiac told them nothing. Their true intelligence came from information they gathered through research, spies, and observations. The prophets claimed the stars had spoken, but they were actually basing their prophecy on what they could see.

Micaiah's vision simply acknowledged the falsehood involved in their pagan belief system, a system of fraud and deceit. The spirit of falsehood had taken residence in their mouths a long before Micaiah's vision and prophecy.

In his final warning, Micaiah sums up the situation nicely. " 'Take heed, all you people', " a caution good for all generations.

Indeed. The honest soul in search of his God must take heed against self-delusion in the spirit of falsehood. He or she must yearn for the truth, look only for the truth, and accept the unaltered truth as he finds it. And, always, the honest searcher must test all words and knowledge for trustworthiness. The one who believes a lie is lost, for falsehoods do not save. In one's search for salvation, truth saves. Lies kill.

Footnotes:

1   Genesis 3:6

2   Future Tense/Past Tense
The ancient Hebrew did not employ past tense. They spoke of past events in the present tense. Young's translated the Hebrew in 1 Kings 22:22 as past tense, which is more accurate than the future tense found in the King James, New King James, and other versions. This allegorical spirit is saying he has already gone out and been a spirit of falsehood in the mouths of the prophets, his is currently doing so, and he will continue to do the same.

3   Herein lay yet another purposeful mistranslation. The KJV and NKJV mistranslated *prautEtos* as *gentleness*. The word translates correctly as meekness, which is the opposite of haughtiness. Meekness hardly means gentleness. Jesus was meek and lowly, and yet he chased the moneychangers out of the temple with a cat o' nine tails. Driving people away from their money with a whip is not an act of gentility or tenderness.

This shift in words was the Catholic's subtle effort to transform the Master from a rough and ready, masculine, darker-skinned Jewish carpenter into a white European, effeminate, namby-pamby, wimp with long stringy hair. The artists certainly depicted him this way in all their paintings throughout the Middle Ages. By the way, this undermines the legitimacy of the Turin Shroud – the image on the shroud is of a Middle Ages, European Caucasian and not of a first century Jew.

4   sparknotes
    https://www.sparknotes.com/lit/animalfarm/symbols

5   Anthropomorphic Personification
    The personification of inanimate objects, giving them human characteristics and or human behaviors, for example, the ability to speak

6   This is No Synagogue! By Simcha Jacobovici
    July 22, 2013
    www.simchajtv.com/this-is-no-synagogue/

These are things we know.
There are things we know we don't know.
There are things we don't know that we don't know.

Donald Rumsfeld

FOUR

THE PREVAILING VIEW

Beyond the religious world's errant understanding of Micaiah's vision, it also holds a misguided view on the Jews' preparation for battle and the battle itself. This misguided view has produced a bit of an irony. While the religious world holds vastly divergent views on any particular subject, it holds a substantially single view on the events portrayed in 1 Kings and Chronicles. It is as if someone many years ago penned his opinion on what these passages meant, and everyone simply adopted his erroneous assertions unquestioned.

All commentators, teachers, and preachers in one voice

basically say:

- Jehoshaphat visits his royal in-law
    - He visits without an agenda
- Ahab asks Jehoshaphat to help him retake Ramoth-Gilead from the Syrians
- Jehoshaphat agrees
- However, being a Godly king, he wants a word from God
- Ahab has his four hundred prophets give their word
- Jehoshaphat, unsatisfied, asks for a prophet of God
- Ahab sends for Micaiah
- Zechariah makes two iron horns and presents them to the two Jewish kings
    - This symbolizes the two kings goring the Syrians
    - (Some say it represents the two Jewish kingdoms)
- Micaiah arrives and gives a good report
    - However, he uses a mocking tone to show he was not telling the truth
    - Because of the mocking, sarcastic tone, the king does not believe
- Micaiah then tells the truth, foretelling Ahab's

death
- Ahab objects to the forecast of his death
- Micaiah reveals a vision
    - A host of spiritual beings in Heaven stand before God's throne
    - God asks who will persuade Ahab to go to Ramoth-Gilead
    - A spirit, either angel or demon, says he would become a lying spirit in the mouths of the prophets
    - God tells the spirit to go do it
- Zechariah slaps Micaiah over the lying spirit thing
- Ahab grows angry at this prophecy and has Micaiah cast into prison
    - Some suggest Ahab was likely sending Micaiah back to prison
- At Ramoth-Gilead, Ahab somehow talks Jehoshaphat into wearing his royal robe while he disguises himself
    - Ahab hides, because he is afraid of Micaiah's death prophecy
    - Some commentators admit they have no idea how Ahab could have talked the King of Judah into taking his place
    - Many commentators simply ignore the logical dilemma

- The king of Syria orders his charioteers to fight only Ahab
  - Some commentators suggest this is what caused Ahab to hide
- These charioteers eventually find Jehoshaphat
  - Believing he is King Ahab, they attack
  - Jehoshaphat cries out in fear
  - God helps Jehoshaphat and directs the Syrian charioteers away from him (Chronicles)
- A random arrow fired by a random archer hits Ahab in his armor's weak spot
- Ahab dies, just as Micaiah prophesied

The Moral: You can't hide from God and or his prophecy

The list above hits the highlights of the religious world's explanation. Their view on this chapter completely misrepresents the events reported in 1 Kings 22. The conclusion is completely off base. The lesson in this chapter is not about a rebellious king running away from God, Jonah like, or hiding from his prophecy. There is a far more important lesson attached to these events. And this lesson, relevant to the people at the date of the writing, about 500 BC, is even more relevant today.

Beyond the mistranslations, the reader struggles with the writer's presentation of the facts. They come in fragments of limited details. The current view is born by speculating the meaning of these information bites. However, speculation does not produce an accurate understanding of the events. Guessing never produces accurate answers.

Nonetheless, these fragments do contain enough information to shed a bright light on what actually happened and what it all means – but only when the reader objectively deduces. Moreover, the biblical student needs to bring to a chapter concerning a battle some external knowledge, specifically information about military protocols and procedures.

The external information is not complicated, difficult to find, or mysterious. The protocols and methodologies Ahab and Jehoshaphat used to fight Benhadad are the same General Norman Schwarzkopf used to defeat Saddam Hussein some three thousand years later.

It is difficult to tell if the readers in 500 BC had as much trouble understanding this chapter. Reading or hearing the account in their native language likely aided comprehension. Also, without suffering the false lessons movies and television teach, it is possible the people possessed a more accurate understanding how an army conducts combat operations. Nonetheless, the necessary information is out there, sometimes just one browser search away.

There is more in this fight for Ramoth-Gilead than the current view appreciates.

When you go out to battle against your enemies and see horses and chariots and people more numerous than you, do not be afraid of them; for the Lord your God, who brought you up from the land of Egypt, is with you.

Deuteronomy 20:1

FIVE

THE TWO PREVIOUS BATTLES

To understand Ahab and Jehoshaphat's military adventure in 1 Kings 22 more fully, it is important to review the two previous military engagements between Ahab and Benhadad. In both, Benhadad traveled to Samaria as the aggressor. Moreover, the Syrian army outnumbered Ahab's dramatically each engagement. Nonetheless, with God's help, Ahab's army thrashed the Syrians both times.

The record of the two previous battles in chapter twenty and the events surrounding them contain information related to the battle for Ramoth-Gilead.

First Battle - 1 Kings 20: 1-22

Benhadad encroached Samaria and positioned his army to attack the city. The Syrian king made certain demands, and Ahab, facing a massively superior force, wisely conceded Benhadad's high and unorthodox ransom. However, the moment Ahab agreed, Benhadad demanded more. After consulting the Elders, the Jewish king balked at paying any of it.

When Ahab refused, Benhadad said, " '...[May] the gods do so to me, and more also, if enough dust is left of Samaria for a handful for each of the people who follow me'." (1 Kings 20: 10)

To this, Ahab said: " 'Tell him [Benhadad], "Let not the one who puts on his armor boast like the one who takes it off'. "

The religious world makes out Ahab was a coward. However, this exchange with Benhadad shows the king had spit and vinegar. This is not the kind of man to hide from danger.

Now, about this time, an unnamed, unannounced

prophet appeared:

> "Suddenly a prophet approached Ahab king of Israel, saying, 'Thus says the Lord: "Have you seen all this great multitude? Behold, I will deliver it into your hand today, and you shall know that I am the Lord". ' So Ahab said, 'By whom?' And he said, 'Thus says the Lord: "By the young leaders of the provinces". ' Then he said, 'Who will set the battle in order?' And he answered, 'You.' Then he mustered the young leaders of the provinces, and there were two hundred and thirty-two; and after them he mustered all the people, all the children of Israel – seven thousand." (1 Kings 20: 13-15)

The next passages read awkwardly. But, after reviewing the text in a number of translations, including the literal, the following is a fairly accurate rendition.

The Syrian army was positioned to attack. However, while Benhadad and Ahab sent messages back and forth, the Syrian king had his army rest in place. Meanwhile, and rather unconcerned about the Jewish army, the Syrian king and the thirty-two royal commanders of his chariot forces drank. It appears they drank themselves drunk.

Now, upon Ahab's final message, Benhadad ordered his troops to stand ready. Meanwhile, Ahab sent out the two hundred thirty-two young men. Benhadad's scouts sent word a group of men were coming out of the city. Benhadad sent word back, telling the scouts to arrest the group no matter their intent, peaceful or belligerent. When the scouts attempted to apprehend the little group, the band of Jews engaged and killed the scouts as seven thousand Jewish warriors poured out of the city.

Now, the Jewish battle plan followed an interesting strategy, which no commander should employ unless he has no other choice. Its success depended heavily upon the enemy's reaction to a surprise attack. If the Syrians had reacted contrary to expectation, if they had not run, the Jews could have streamed out of the city into a terrible mess. Nonetheless, the prophet told him to do it, and Ahab did. It is interesting a rebellious king would actually obey the prophet's instruction. Nonetheless, the slaughter of scouts and sudden surge of Jewish troops appears to have caught the Syrian army wholly off guard and sent a chill through the ranks.

Suddenly afraid, they fled. This flight was apparently

disorderly, the opposite of a fighting withdrawal. Of course, the drunken royals likely exacerbated their mobbish retreat. As the Jews pursued the fleeing Syrians, Benhadad escaped on horseback with some of his cavalry.

Ahab's forces attacked the Syrian chariots, doing a good deal of damage. It is not absolutely clear, but it appears Ahab captured a large number of these chariots and horses. Of course, a gaggle of intoxicated kings in charge of the Syrian chariots would have diminished their ability to resist the Jews. This, and the mass confusion would have left Ahab's footed forces free to do as they pleased, capture and or destroy.

Later in the chapter, the reader discovers the Syrian chariot force had found it difficult to maneuver in Samaria's hill country. This difficulty and the intoxication would have made it double easy for foot soldiers to capture or damage the Syrian chariot force. All things considered, it appears Ahab captured more than he destroyed. And, the chariots Ahab captured are likely the same ones he employed in the following battle and the battle for Ramoth-Gilead.

After the fight, the same prophet appeared and warned

Ahab the Syrians would return: " 'Go, strengthen yourself; take note, and see what you should do, for in the spring of the year the king of Syria will come up against you'. " (1 Kings 20:22)

Important Note: Ahab did not call for a prophet. The unnamed prophet simply appeared and gave him God's word of victory and returned with a warning of a spring attack.

The Second Battle - 1 Kings 20: 23-34

Back in Syria, Benhadad licked his wounds and rebuilt his forces:

> "Then the servants of the king of Syria said to him, 'Their gods are gods of the hills. Therefore they were stronger than we; but if we fight against them in the plain, surely we will be stronger than they. So do this thing: Dismiss the kings, each from his position, and put captains in their places; and you shall muster an army like the army that you have lost, horse for horse and chariot for chariot. Then we will fight against them in the plain; surely we will be stronger than they'. " (1 Kings 20:23-25)

Notice the importance of chariots to the Syrian army. Chariot and or cavalry forces were key to victory. To this day, mobile forces are one of the most important elements in an army.

So, Benhadad's pagan aids read the tea leaves and declared God a pagan god of the hills. Therefore, they advised Benhadad should fight Ahab in the plain, where his god is greater than God.

While this sounds like a load of pagan nonsense, and it is, it is also sound military advice. Chariot forces operate better in the flat, where they are free to maneuver unobstructed. Of course, God did not overlook the Syrian's blasphemy. It motivated him to support Ahab a second time.

Dismissing the kings was also sound military advice. Royals are not necessarily adept at following orders. These also were, as reported, not above drinking on the job. Military captains, on the other hand, are better suited to following commands and are less likely to get drunk before a fight.

It is important to note how the writer, Jeremiah,

interjected important military information into his historical account. He continued this in 1 Kings 22.

That spring, Benhadad marched his rebuilt army to Samaria. The script says the Jewish force looked like two little flocks of goats against the massive Syrian force, which filled the countryside.

The script then reports a second man suddenly appeared. The script calls this fellow a "man of God." There is no difference between prophet and man of God. For example, the writer of 2 Kings 6 repeatedly labeled the prophet Elisha a "man of God". Nonetheless, the change in terminology here in 1 Kings 20 implies the first and second men may have been different fellows, both bringing nearly identical messages – victory against a vastly superior force.

This fellow, like the prophet before, gave Ahab a good report. Ahab would win. This time, however, the prophet tells Ahab God was aiding him, because Benhadad's aids had disparaged him. Then, as in the first prophet's message, he said God was also aiding Ahab to show he was the Lord – a lesson Ahab never really seemed to learn.

The text does not record much about the battle except the two armies encamped across from one another for seven days, somewhat reminiscent of the Jews' seven-day march around Jericho.

Now, it would seem Benhadad's superior force should have immediately surrounded and crushed Ahab's little army. However, they did not. Maybe Benhadad was leery of God's people, who had earlier whipped him soundly with an inferior force. Maybe Ahab had positioned his army in a way the Syrians could not maneuver their chariot forces. The script does not say.

Whatever the reason, on the day the two sides engaged in battle, the tiny Jewish force devastated the massive Syrian army, killing one hundred thousand foot soldiers. The rest fled to Aphek, a nearby city. The text says a wall then fell on twenty-seven thousand of the fleeing Syrian soldiers.

> Yet, another important point: Before Ramoth-Gilead, Ahab was feeling fairly confident about his chances for victory. Defeating a massive force with a handful of warriors can go to a man's head. His history suggests he did not

acknowledge he had won through God's power and not on his own. This kind of attitude fairly sums up the man's life.

This wall thing is rather odd. It seems to defy logic for a single wall to fall on so many men. However, consider the following possibility: Walled cities had ramparts, a place on top to stand and fight an attacking enemy force.

The translations record "a wall fell on twenty-seven thousand men." The Hebrew word, *echume*, is better translated as *the wall*. This wall was likely the entire city wall enclosing the town.

If the terrified, fleeing soldiers were to mount this rampart with too many soldiers, they could have collapsed the wall on themselves, on the soldiers climbing up the walls, and on the mass of soldiers waiting to climb. If this wall had a flaw in its foundation, either by design, age, or water damage, the extra weight could easily have triggered its downfall.

Here's a thing about ancient prepositions. English has a preposition for every occasion, on, over, under, with, beside, atop, inside, outside, up, down, in, out, etc, etc,

etc. Ancient Hebrew and Greek apparently multitasked prepositions. So, the same preposition serves as both *on* and *with*. The translators likely did not fully understand what they read in the original language and chose the word *on*. Whatever the terminology, the falling wall killed twenty-seven thousand frightened, fleeing soldiers.

After this battle, the Syrian king did not flee with his horsemen but took refuge in the city, hiding in an inner room. He attempted to avoid the Jews but managed only to avoid the collapsing wall.

Now, Ahab failed to dispatch Benhadad as God had ordered. Instead, he made a treaty with the Syrian king for the return of certain cities the Benhadad's father had previously taken, including Ramoth-Gilead. Then, Ahab simply let him go.

Lions and Prophets and Bears - 1 Kings 20: 35-43

After the battle, another unnamed prophet, likely a third, told a companion by word of the Lord to strike him, presumably in the head. The fellow refused, which resulted in another unusual occurrence. The unnamed prophet declared, " 'Because you have not obeyed the voice of the Lord, surely, as soon as you depart from me, a lion shall kill you'. And as soon as he left him, a lion found him and killed him." (Verse 36)

The Lion

According to the Apostle John, his gospel did not record every event in Jesus's life: "And there are also many other things that Jesus did, which if they were written one by one, I suppose that even the world itself could not contain the books that would be written." (John 21:25)

Likewise, the Old Testament did not record every aspect of every event. Therefore, Jeremiah's inclusion of the lion indicates the incident has a meaning deeper than the simple fact a lion slaughtered a disobedient prophet.

Scripture is holographic. Pieces from different places connect to form a complete picture. An event in one section of the bible often has a relationship with an event in another. In this, Jeremiah's book of Kings reports three incidents of lions killing disobedient people, two prophets and one group of rebellious Jews.

In 1 Kings 13, God told a young prophet to go

prophesy against Israel's false altar. However, he was not to eat or drink in Israel. He was also to take a different route back home to Judah. He disobeyed, and a lion killed him. Thereafter, it stood by the body along with the donkey the prophet had ridden. (Verses 11-32)

In 1 Kings 20, the unnamed man of God ordered one of the sons of the prophets to strike him by word of the Lord. The fellow refused. "…as soon as he left him, a lion found him and killed him." (1 Kings 20:36)

In 2 Kings 17, the Jews displaced in Assyria had adopted a plethora of local pagan religious practices, including worshiping the stars and Baal. They placed sacred pillars on every high hill and wooden images under every green tree. "And it was so, at the beginning of their dwelling there, that they did not fear the Lord; therefore the Lord sent lions among them, which killed some of them. (2 Kings 17:25)

A similar event occurred with bears. In 2 Kings 2, young men began mocking Elisha: " 'Go up, you baldhead! Go up, you baldhead!' " So he pronounced a curse on them in the name of the Lord, and two female bears appeared and mauled forty-two of the youths'. " (Verses 23, 24)

In the first incident, a prophet did what God said don't do, and a lion killed him.

In the second incident, a prophet did not do what God said to do, and a lion killed him.

In the third, the people did what God said don't and did not what God said do, and God sent multiple lions to kill a number of them.

In the bear incident, mocking God's prophet is mocking God's word, which is mocking God. Few beasts equal the viciousness of a sow bear.

The book of Kings records all four events. This makes sense, in that the prophet Jeremiah is the apparent writer of the book. The book of Kings is not just a history but also a prophecy told through the historical account.

Jeremiah's use of symbolism is not unusual. In his book, fire represents the Messiah. For example, the fire coming down from the heavens at Mount Carmel consumed the sacrifice, wood, stones, and water. It even erased the dirt, upon which the altar sat. This foreshadowed Jesus's sacrifice at Calvary, which, as the perfect sacrifice, consumed and removed the practice forever.

Likewise, as fire in the Old Testament represents the Messiah, the lions also represent him. This same Jesus, our savior and advocate, is also judge. As the judge, he will on that day sentence the disobedience to spiritual death. More immediately, the prophet-killing lion in 1 Kings 20 foreshadowed the king's price for disobedience, punctuating the prophet's later warning.

> "Thus says the Lord: 'Because you [Ahab] have let slip out of your hand a man whom I appointed to utter destruction, therefore your life shall go for his life, and your people for his people.'" (1 Kings 20:42)

Among all these events stands an interesting lesson in 1 Kings 13's symbolism. The donkey's presence shows the lion intended to kill the young prophet only. The lion's behavior is in direct contrast to the young prophet, the reluctant prophet, and Ahab's four hundred prophets. While these men did not obey God's mandates, the lion, in strict obedience to God's will, ignored its powerful instinct to kill and eat the donkey. Likewise, the donkey, which should have run from the lion in fear, stayed in obedience.

Also, consider another lesson in 1 Kings 13. The young prophet could not use the old prophet's tricky lie as an excuse, a thing Adam tried back in the Garden. Paul wrote in Galatians 1:8, 9 to beware of anyone preaching a gospel other than what he preached. If a false teacher's false lesson lures a listener into error, the subverting teacher and the subverted student are both subject to judgment.

It's up to the individual to distinguish truth from deceit. Sadly, this requires more dedicated study than most people give to any subject. Nonetheless, the dedicated student must diligently verify everything, words, word phrases, ideals, ideas, beliefs, and notions.

This isn't a casual thing. Biblical study isn't reading instructions on how to construct a chair from a build-it-yourself store. We're talking about one's everlasting soul, which, if disqualified, will not see paradise. Best to double check to make sure which beliefs are born of God's truth and which are the products of Satan's lies.

Again in 2 Corinthians 11:12-15, Paul wrote, "But what I do, I will also continue to do, that I may cut off the opportunity from those who desire an opportunity to be regarded just as we are in the things of which they boast. For such are false apostles, deceitful workers, transforming themselves into apostles of Christ. And no wonder! For Satan himself transforms himself into an angel of light. Therefore it is no great thing if his ministers also transform themselves into ministers of righteousness, whose end will be according to their works."

Jesus put it a little more succinctly. " 'Beware of false prophets, who come to you in sheep's clothing, but inwardly they are ravenous wolves'. " (Matthew 7:15)

Don't follow Ahab and Jehoshaphat's example. Beware, beware, beware.

Summation

The son of the prophet not striking the unnamed prophet stands as a type-antitype to Zechariah slapping Micaiah over the spirit of falsehood comment. While the son of the prophets was not spared due to a momentary defiance, the ungodly man, who lives a life of rebellion, will also suffer. Who can resist God and his message?

In like manner, these first two battles stand as a preamble to Ahab's third battle over Ramoth-Gilead. Some particulars in these first two battles reflect directly on the third in three specific areas.

1. A prophet and a man of God appeared uninvited before both battles to give Ahab good news of victory. Before Ramoth-Gilead, no prophet suddenly appeared, which is likely what prompted Jehoshaphat to ask.

2. A son of the prophet did not strike the unnamed prophet and suffered punishment. Zechariah struck Micaiah and suffered his king's defeat.

3. Benhadad hid from the Jews after the battle, an incident to which Micaiah alludes after Zechariah slaps him.

4. The captured chariots are essential in the battle over Ramoth-Gilead.

Also, in the account of these two previous battles, the writer made sure to mention the pagan advisors' sound military advice, such as their suggestion Benhadad replace the thirty-two royals with captains. Jeremiah, through knowledge and purpose, included the military aspects of the events into his historical record.

It is important to recognize these military interjects. He includes this information throughout his accounts of all three battles. This is not an accident. These are there to fill the gaps in the brief account. Nonetheless, the reader must possess at least a little military knowledge to fully comprehend the events depicted. Without it, there is no way to fully appreciate what the two Jewish kings were up to before the battle or understand the amazing ploy they pulled on Benhadad in the battle over Ramoth-Gilead.

Finally, as in any military campaign, there's always the unexpected. The wall falling on the twenty-seven thousand soldiers was surely a huge surprise. A random arrow striking King Ahab in a chink in his armor would have equally caught the Jews off guard. Human beings have a difficult time with the unexpected.

Nobody sees it coming, nobody but God.

In an attack, you should have a ratio of approximately three to one in favor of the attacker.

General Norman Schwarzkopf

SIX

CHESS AND THE BATTLEFIELD FORMATION

All kings and commanders fight and have fought wars according to protocols developed through the years. A battle may look like a chaotic free-for-all, but unless something has gone terribly wrong, it is far from disorganized. The ancient battle for Ramoth-Gilead is no exception. To fully understand the battle over Ramoth-Gilead, the reader needs to possess at least a little knowledge in battlefield formations, tactics, and strategies.

A disorganized army will lose the fight. All armies go into battle with a plan and in formation. Some formations are complicated. Some are simpler. All formations adapt to terrain and the commander's plan. Since the territory around Ramoth-Gilead is flat and open, the battle formations the Jews and Syrian's employed were likely rather straightforward.

The game of chess well demonstrates the standard battlefield formation. The chessboard example helps explain much about 1 Kings 22. Although the battle at Ramoth-Gilead took place around 850 BC, modern battlefield commanders employ the same formations, tactics, and strategies. The war to oust Saddam Hussein from Kuwait stands as a good illustration of how an intelligent general deploys his army according to military protocols. Moreover, the general in this war, General Norman Schwarzkopf, employed a couple of clever tricks, ruses equal to the subterfuge Ahab and Jehoshaphat had used against Benhadad.

Chess and The Battlefield

A commander or king does not allow his army to run about willy-nilly, attacking here or there. All armies fight as one in a formation. A structured formation focuses the army's efforts and facilitates the command's ability to coordinate movements, directing who does what, when, where, and why.

In this, the basic formation presents a frontline with the commander behind it. The mobile forces guard the flank or flanks. All battle formations, past and present, follow this fundamental pattern.

The modern chessboard is based upon an idealized battlefield formation with additional pieces, bishops, queens, and rooks.

Remove the superfluous pieces, and the chessboard represents the basic ancient battle formation, a frontline, the king centered behind the frontline, and a mobile force positioned left and or right.

Idealized battle formation for any period in history, frontlines, mobile forces left and right, and king (commanders) in the rear.

Due to military necessities, battle formations do not always create perfect formations according to the chessboard example. Terrain often dictates shape. Sometimes, the line curves, such as seen along the Kuwait/Saudi border during Gulf War I. Sometimes the cavalry guards only one flank when impassable terrain hedges the other. The Persian Gulf, for example, prevented allied mobile forces from flanking Hussein's left.

With all this in mind, the area around modern Ramoth-Gilead is rather open and flat. So, this book will treat the battle formation at Ramoth-Gilead according to the chessboard example, on level ground without obstructions.

Cavalry / Chariot Forces

When Americans think of a cavalry, they envision John Wayne and the 7th patrolling the Four Corners region. In the Civil War before the Indians Wars, military units mostly coordinated cavalry movements with frontline troops. However, facing the Indians of the American west, the most effective horse-mounted guerrilla fighters in military history, the 7th and others had to often operate independently. It was the only way to chase down the rapid mobile warriors. Cavalry units throughout history have proven themselves flexible and adaptable.

In a battle formation, both cavalries and chariots perform similar roles. There are advantages and disadvantages to each, and ancient armies often employed both. Above all other considerations, their flexibility and mobility were their greatest strengths. Foot soldiers can move only so far so fast. Compared to horses, mounted or charioted, they are relatively clumsy. A cavalry or chariot force can travel over thirty miles-per-hour for a distance and half that speed for a number of miles. No foot soldier can match a horse's performance.

In a battle, ancient and modern, mobile forces perform

two important roles. They use their speed and mobility to outflank the enemy. Since an opposing mobile force is the only element fast and agile enough to match this kind of mobility, a mobile forces' second role is to block enemy mobile forces from outflanking its own army.

Schwarzkopf's mechanized forces showed the flanking maneuver is still an important military maneuver. The massive American mobile force outflanked Hussein's entire army. If Hussein had known what he was doing, he would have set his own mechanized force to guard his right flank. Of course, this never occurred to the Iraqi leader.

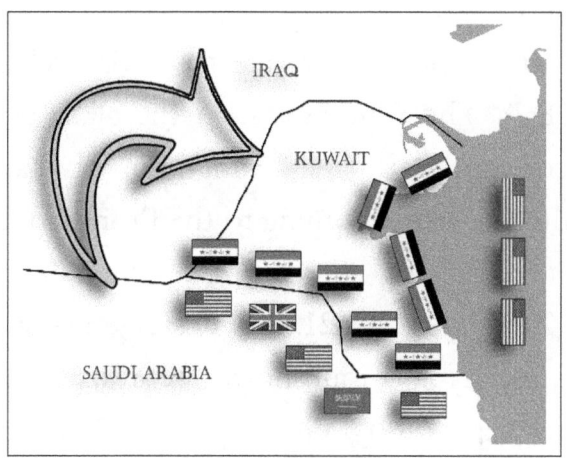

Horn / Horns

In the Bible, horns symbolically represent a number of things. The horns in Daniel represent both individual kings and groups of kings. The goat with one horn is obviously Alexander the Great. The ram's two horns represent all the kings of the Medes and all the kings of Persia.

Horns also represent power, as in Deuteronomy 33:17 "

'His glory is like a firstborn bull, and his horns like the horns of the wild ox; together with them he shall push the peoples to the ends of the earth…' " This passage is a metaphor, renaming a thing by reflection, signified by the word *like*.

Also, horns represent salvation (2 Samuel 22:3 and Psalm 18:2). The four horns on the altar, pointing to four corners of the kingdom, metaphorically represented salvation coming to the Promised Land.

Also, in Zechariah 1:18-21, the messenger showed God's prophet, Zechariah, four horns, representing the four kingdoms suppressing God's people. Then he shows him four craftsmen (Hebrew = *chrshim*: artificers, stone carvers, tapestry makers, metal workers, etc). These craftsmen would terrify the four horns and cast them out.

Lately, some people made an errant connection between the above passage in the book, Zechariah, and the false prophet Zechariah's presentation of iron horns in 1 Kings 22, claiming the horns in Zechariah's prophecy were iron, because the metalworker craftsmen would pound them with hammers or some such nonsense.

This errant connection is a good example of linking symbols without cause. Similarity does not always mean two things are connected. The symbolism in the book of Zechariah has nothing to do with the false prophet's horns in Kings. God's prophet, Zechariah, used his horns to forecast the rebuilding of the temple (Zechariah 2), of which the craftsmen played a pivotal role. With the temple back, God again sat in the Holy of Holies. This then led to the savior's arrival, which led to his taking " 'away the filthy garments." That is, Jesus, as high priest, would remove iniquity and clothe the saved in rich robes. (Zechariah 3:4)

The craftsmen in the Godly prophet's metaphor do not make, shape, or flatten horns. They terrified the horns by building the temple. The horns in the craftsmen prophecy are not iron. Iron is nowhere in the Bible used to represent kings. By claiming the horns in the craftsmen prophecy are iron is to speak beyond the script. It also wholly misses the prophet's point, which is a prophecy of the coming salvation through Lord Jesus.

The connection between iron and horns in 1 Kings 22 and 2 Chronicles 18 is unique in the Bible, limited to this one incident.

Horns And the Flanking Maneuver

The use of horns to represent a chariot force's flanking maneuver is neither novel nor unique. Two good examples are Genghis Khan's horns tactic and Shaka Zulu's bull horn formation.

According to Michiko Phifer:

> "Genghis Khan employed a rudimentary form of the pincer movement, known colloquially as the horns tactic. In his version, two enveloping flanks of horsemen surrounded the enemy. However, they usually did not close the circle, leaving the enemy a backdoor escape route. Khan's use of this tactic was key to many of his early victories over other Mongolian tribes." (Edited)[1]

This and other tactics gave Khan victory after victory. Later, in the early eighteen hundreds, Shaka kaSenzangakhona, also known as Shaka Zulu, ruled his kingdom as the greatest military thinker in all Sub Saharan Africa. He did not study Western battle formations, tactics, and strategies. He was born in the land cut off from foreign knowledge. A Western military education was unavailable to him. Nonetheless, the man had an innate understanding of military maneuvers. He realized the value of the flanking maneuver without having seen it elsewhere used.

Tribes in Africa at that time fought battles by basically crashing fighting units into one another. Battles fought in this fashion usually end in a draw, especially between armies of equal size and abilities. This was of little consequence to the Africans. These folks fought mostly to vent frustrations. They did not necessarily intend to win territories or capture peoples. Shaka Zulu changed the rules. Using superior formations, tactics, and strategies, he made himself the region's most powerful ruler through military conquest.

Two innovations gave Shaka the upper hand, the bull horn formation and his use of a ready reserve (also called bull's horns or buffalo horns formation). Shaka's formation broke down into three parts: the horns, the head, and the loins. Anyone who saw the movie, Zulu, with Michael Cane will remember the Afrikaner character, Lieutenant Gert Adendorff, describing this formation to the two British officers.

"It looks jolly simple, doesn't it?"

"It's jolly deadly, ol' boy."

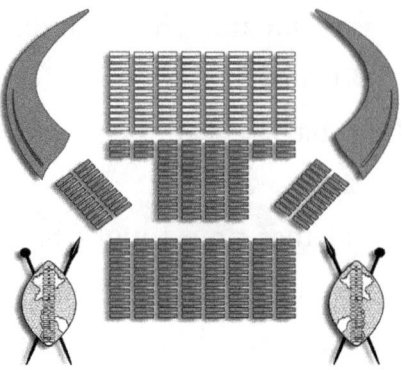

Although generally accurate, the movie misrepresented exactly how the Zulus used their battle formation. This is why one should not glean his or her education through movies and television programs.

Notwithstanding, the head of Shaka's bull horn was the main body. The frontline of this head consisted of older, more experienced warriors. Their job was to engage and pin the enemy down in battle. The horns, consisting of younger, faster warriors, formed up left and right of the head as part of the main force. The loins were a ready reserve, trailing the head. This reserve pulled double duty. They stood by, available to leap into battle if needed. They also guarded against sneak attacks.

Other tribes never thought to outflank the enemy. They

also did not usually hold a force in reserve. Either the horn formation or the ready reserve alone would have given Shaka the edge. The combination of the two made his army invincible.

Although the Zulu formation utilized the same tactics as armies with cavalries and chariot forces, horses did not exist in black Africa. The Zulu king instead made do with his younger, fleet-footed soldiers.

Iron Horns

Zechariah made horns of iron and presented them to his king. Due to the link between horns and kings in Daniel's prophecy and Deuteronomy 33:17, many biblical commentators naturally conclude the horns represent the two kings, Ahab and Jehoshaphat. Some claim they represent the two kingdoms. However, this assertion has a couple of problems. First, the script does not say how many horns Zechariah presented. And, iron is nowhere in the Bible symbolically linked with kings. The only linkage is Daniel's statue, which had legs of iron and feet of iron and clay. This iron, however, symbolizes a specific kingdom, Rome, a one-off connection found only in the Book of Daniel.

However, several biblical passages specifically connect iron with chariots:

- Joshua 17:16 "…the Canaanites who dwell in the land of the valley have chariots of iron…"
- Joshua 17:18 "…they have iron chariots and are strong."
- Judges 1:19 "…because they had chariots of iron."
- Judges 4:3 / 4:13 "…nine hundred chariots of iron…"

Zechariah's iron horns did not represent the kings or their kingdoms. They represented the chariot forces. His language reveals this, for he did not say the kings would gore the enemy. He said:

> " **'With these** you shall gore the Syrians until they are destroyed'. " (1 Kings 22:11, emphasis mine)

The word phrase, "with these," does not refer to the two kings. They would not have used themselves to gore the enemy. They would not have used their kingdoms to gore the enemy. He was saying the kings would use the thing the iron horns represented to gore the Syrians, their chariot forces.

Additionally, if the Jews and Syrians liked up their battlefield formations according to the chessboard example, then the Jewish chariot forces divided into four elements. Zechariah could have easily presented four horns to represent them. The script simply says "horns".

Chariot Forces of Equal Size

As mentioned earlier, military forces of equal size and ability tend to fight to a draw, canceling each other out. Chariot forces of equal size also tend to cancel each other by fighting to a draw.

Due to the three years of peace and Benhadad's order to his charioteers at Ramoth-Gilead, it appears Ahab and Benhadad's chariot forces had reached an equilibrium or near equilibrium of size and ability during the three-year period. Kings ordinarily refrained from fighting battles destined to end in a draw. By joining Ahab, Jehoshaphat likely doubled Ahab's army. The addition of Jehoshaphat's chariots also likely made Ahab's chariot forces twice Benhadad's. With such numbers, the Jews could have blocked Benhadad's chariots with half their force and outflanked the Syrian army unmolested with the remainder.

White has twice gray's chariot force

White blocks gray's chariots with half its chariots

The Counter To A Superior Chariot Force

If Benhadad faced a mobile force twice his chariot force's size, he had a problem. Half the Jew's chariots could block his entire chariot force while the rest outflanked his army. This situation is untenable.

As an experienced warrior king, son and grandson of warrior kings, Benhadad was well trained in the art and craft of warfare. Benhadad knew just what to do against a chariot force larger than his own. The Syrian's order defines his solution. " 'Fight with no one small or great, but only with the king of Israel'. " (Verse 31)

Now, consider the chessboard formation model below. The nature of this battlefield formation creates a problem for such an order. How can one chariot force outflank the other without engaging the enemy's chariot forces?

On the surface, it might seem Benhadad had given a command his charioteers could not possibly obey. This is where a little knowledge of military tactics comes into play.

The Syrian's order makes verse 31 the most significant in the chapter, for it shapes the entire battle. It even shapes the two Jewish kings' preparation for the battle.

Alexander the Great's second battle with Darius helps explain Benhadad's order. Long after Ramoth-Gilead, Alexander faced a similar situation when he fought the Persians. The Persian army outnumbered his force at least three to one. Some historians put the numbers around six to one. Alexander could not attempt a flanking maneuver. Darius would have simply blocked Alexander's cavalry with a fraction of his thirty-thousand-strong chariot force while sending the rest to outflank the Greek's smaller army.

To avoid this, Alexander devised a plan to reach King Darius through a hole in the Persian frontline with a novel take on an ancient tactic. Through positioning, he stretched Darius's frontline, weakening the center. Alexander then tricked Darius into opening a hole by moving half his frontline to his right. Once the gap was wide enough, Alexander flooded through with his cavalry. This cavalry charge terrified the Persian king, who freaked and fled.

Five hundred years after the battle for Ramoth-Gilead, Alexander could have given an order to his cavalry identical to Benhadad's: Fight no man, great or small, but Darius, king of Persia.

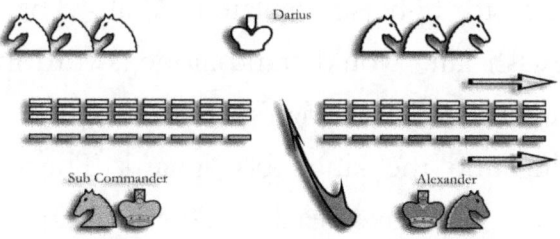

The Battle of Gaugamela included a wedge formation. However, Alexander did not use it to bust through the line but only to exploit the gap already created.

Historians have well documented Alexander's battle with Darius. However, the account of the battle at Ramoth-Gilead is rather sparsely detailed. We have no specific information about their movements. Nonetheless, the Syrian charioteers did reach Jehoshaphat, and there is only one way they could have done so. The Syrian army had to punch a hole in the frontline, and the only way to do so was with a wedge formation. Then, the Syrian chariots could pass through without fighting anyone.

> Important Note: In ancient battles, the king was the most important participant. He did not, therefore, stand alone behind the frontline. Bodyguards escorted ancient kings in battle,

during which these guards and additional soldiers would have set up a defensive perimeter around their monarch. So, Benhadad was not ordering his men to fight an isolated Ahab. The idea the Jewish king would stand alone, sword in hand, is ludicrous. The Syrian's order meant to fight the king and the king's bodyguard. The charioteers could not have reached Ahab without engaging his protection.

Punching a hole in frontlines with a wedge formation is a tactic kings have used for millennia. Armies still use it today, especially when dealing with overwhelming forces. With a gap in the frontline, an ancient chariot force did not need to battle its way to the enemy king. It simply passed through the hole and rushed him.

Certainly, the vagueness of the script reads as if the Syrian chariots wandered about the battlefield like a band of tumbleweeds, looking for an opportunity to strike. This is not the case. They could not have simply meandered around. The Jews would not have left them to drift aimlessly.

When a smaller force meets a larger, the wedge formation gives the inferior force a tactical advantage.

Alexander knew this and pulled his maneuver on the Persian king through tactics and trickery. Nonetheless, the two situations are similar, their intentions identical.

Wedge Formations Yesterday and Today

Most people know this wedge formation in association with the Roman army, which used it to perfection. Notwithstanding, all armies have used wedge formations from time immemorial to create holes in the frontlines of enemy forces.

In a wedge formation, a group of soldiers form into the shape of a wedge, pointed end toward the enemy. The soldiers along the leading edges of this formation overlapped their shields. The soldiers inside could hold their shields overhead as protection from flying arrows and thrown objects. To advance, the soldiers, grouped tightly together, push off with one foot and step forward with the other. This stagger-step gait generates a lot of force.

A wedge formation pushing into the frontline is nearly impossible to stop. Then, once the wedge has penetrated, the soldiers would split in half, turn left and right, and push to widen the gap. With enough effort, the hole can be permanent. However, the enemy will likely regroup, push back, and reseal the hole. Nonetheless, one way or another, the hole would be open long enough for mobile forces and or foot soldiers to flow through unimpeded.

The former Soviet Union devised a modern version of the wedge formation against NATO. Instead of punching a single hole, they planned to punch a series of holes along the frontline, through which tanks and mobile infantry could flow. Once through, the Soviets intended to surround and crush the enclaves. The Soviet plan was a mixture of Benhadad's wedge formation and Shaka's bull horn.

Chess and the Battlefield Formation

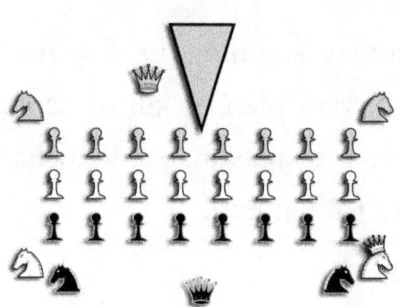

The Syrian Plan Versus a Royal Trick

Since Jehoshaphat standing in for Ahab would have subverted the Syrian plan to kill or capture the king of the battle, then it is reasonable Jehoshaphat and Ahab switched places to that end.

The two Jewish royals, as warrior kings, knew the score. They would have studied Benhadad's military habits. They would have known how the Syrian king responded to superior numbers. They would have realized he would likely employ a wedge formation. They would have known this back in Samaria. They and the Jewish-pagan prophets, who kept a finger on the pulse of events, would have known. Everyone would have known.

Replacing Ahab with Jehoshaphat was not to allow Ahab escape death or capture. The commentators have gotten it wrong. Ahab was not hiding in fear from God's prophecy. The Jews were pulling a royal trick on Benhadad, luring the Syrian charioteers into a death trap. Jehoshaphat was the bait, an illusion of Ahab but not Ahab.

So, let's speculate for a moment. Let's say I've got two independent armies, led by two kings. I position them so the enemy sees only one large army. I know Benhadad will attempt a wedge formation. So, I present an illusion of Ahab, with which I entice their chariots through the line. Doing so separates the Syrian chariots from the Syrian main force. Meanwhile, I send Ahab, the key player as king of the battle, to lead his flanking chariot maneuver around the Syrians.

Once the Syrian chariots are repositioned on the wrong side of things, I can then separate the two Jewish armies. With one, I surround the Syrian charioteers. With the other, I surround the Syrian king and his frontline. The Syrians, now divided, haven't long to survive, each half fighting an entire independent army led by an independent king. The chariot forces are the second key to this plan, which move quickly enough to both trap the Syrian chariots and surround the Syrian main force. Once done, the Jewish chariots can gore the Syrians to destruction.

Chess and the Battlefield Formation

These two Jewish kings were definitely not afraid. Of course Jehoshaphat would present his royal self as bait. Having two kings and two armies was a delicious situation. It allowed the Jews to trick and crush Benhadad. It was a clever royal trick, good enough to cost Benhadad everything.

Although in disguise from the Syrians, Ahab would not have hidden from his own soldiers. He would have worn something to distinguish himself, some such thing the Syrians would have not have automatically considered kingly. A unique plumage would have been good enough. With such a minor distinction, the Syrians would have taken Ahab as just another commander.

Keep in mind, the two Jewish armies certainly recognized Ahab as king of the battle when he died. Therefore, then they would have also recognized him during the fight.

Reading 1 Kings 22 with a little military knowledge while viewing the clues as a whole, the three years of peace, Zechariah's iron horns, Benhadad's order to his charioteers, and Jehoshaphat wearing the royal robes while Ahab fought disguise – all these things combine to create a clear picture of the battle plan, its execution, and the royal trick.

All in all, if Alexander, Schwarzkopf, Patton, and George C. Scott were to consult the plan, they all would have given Ahab and Jehoshaphat the go-ahead. The situation and plan were perfect. There is no way they could lose.

Well, there is always the unexpected.

False Prophets, Soothsayers, And Magicians

Ancient astronomers, soothsayers, seers, magicians, and false prophets all claimed and still claim a connection with the spiritual. Through this lie, the false prophets of old touted themselves able to forecast future events.

Of course, this system of foreknowledge is flawed. Nebuchadnezzar proved this in Babylon, when he demanded his court oracles both tell him his dream and interpret its meaning. As expected, they couldn't. They had no special insight. Like the bones in Willow, pagan icons told pagans phonies nothing. (Daniel 2:1-12)

To make predictions in the ancient past, the court mystics, soothsayers, false prophets, and the like needed information. First, they studied the world around them. Second, they kept a careful eye on current events and the situation at hand. They needed a variety of intelligence to make predictions, interpret dreams, and advise the king. By demanding insight, Nebuchadnezzar caught his magicians on the hop. They desperately needed to know the dream before they could conjure an answer. If they had insight, they would have insight. Of course, they had nothing. Paganism is a pretense of reality, a figment of men's imagination.

To make accurate predictions, Ahab's four hundred prophets, while reading the stars, would have also studied military protocols. They would have watched each situation in the moment, utilizing a network of spies and informants to provide them additional information to fill the gaps. Without these things, they could have never made educated predictions of future events.

It was the same for Benhadad's pagan aids. While they jibber-jabbered about gods of the hills and gods of the valleys, their solid military advice revealed their studied knowledge. They clearly understood military operations, protocols, and methodologies.

This military insight underscores Micaiah's spirit of falsehood allegory. Ahab's prophets did not foresee future events through the zodiac. They prophesied future events according to what they could see. All the things they saw suggested the Jews would win the battle, especially Ahab and Jehoshaphat's plan to lure the Syrians into a trap by having the king of Judah stand as an illusion of Ahab.

Anyone knowledgeable in military affairs would have seen the same and advised the Jews to go. Ahab had the right army with the right plan and the right trick at the right time. The battle was his to lose.

In the end, the decision to go belonged to Ahab and Jehoshaphat. The four hundred prophets encouraged them, but these two kings also believed what they saw with their eyes as they ignored God's disapproving word. In the grand scheme of things, they believed their finite eyes over what the infinite God had said.

This is still a problem today.

The Modern Battlefield

In 1991, General Norman Schwarzkopf, as leader of the

coalition forces, pushed Saddam Hussein out of Kuwait. The Iraqis fielded the fourth largest army in the world. So, the general held back until the buildup of allied forces was sufficient. Once accomplished, and after shooting down and chasing off the entire Iraqi air force, the American-led forces drove Saddam out of Kuwait in only one hundred hours of combat.

Now, the general spent his career studying battlefield formations, tactics, strategies, and tricks. Meanwhile, Saddam Hussein had clearly studied nothing. Hussein may have played military commander in a spiffy uniform, beret, and gold adorned epaulets, but he didn't know a thing about conducting military campaigns.

This did not go unnoticed. The American general came to the Middle East fully aware the Iraqi leadership lacked this necessary military knowledge. He and the US military studied the eight-year-long conflict between Iraq and Iran, a war well demonstrating both sides suffered a complete lack of military know-how.

Interestingly, the lack of knowledge was self-inflicted. When Hussein took over Iraq, he killed, deported, and chased off all his generals for fear they might overthrow him. This created a military brain drain. Likewise, when the Iranian revolutionaries deposed the Shah, they killed, deported, and chased off all the Shah's generals, creating a brain drain equal to Iraq.

So both countries, knowing nothing about conducting major combat operations, basically lined up their two massive armies and crashed them together. Day after day, year after year, the two military forces mauled one other in fruitless combat, wasting lives, equipment, and money. For all their efforts, for all the money and lives spent, they gained absolutely nothing in return.

In the buildup to Gulf War I, the general used Hussein's lack of knowledge against him. First, he massed American, Saudi, and British units on the Saudi side of the Kuwait border. There was no military need to do such a thing. The Americans knew the Iraqis absolutely did not intend to cross the border into Saudi Arabia. Nonetheless, massing soldiers on the border was a trick. The buildup of allied soldiers triggered Hussein into positioning a large portion of his army against the perceived threat.

Of this massive frontline, the allies ended it cold where the Kuwait, Iraq, and Saudi borders all met. The Iraqis, knowing nothing about flanking maneuvers, also ended their frontline at the same place, leaving their right flank wholly exposed.

Now, by tying up a large segment of Saddam's army to guard against an empty threat, the general basically took them out of the fight. This brought him one step closer to his three to one superiority.

The general had also learned Saddam watched CNN for information. It was the dictator's only real source of military intelligence. So, Schwarzkopf invited all news agencies, especially CNN, to cover the Marines as they practiced amphibious landings on a Saudi beach. Hussein saw the landings and, once again, took the bait, massing another large portion of his military on the Kuwait coastline. It was a ploy. The Americans never intended to make an amphibious assault. For the entire war, a mass of Iraqi soldiers hung out on Kuwaiti beaches for phantom Marine hydrofoils.

The general's tricks were sublime. With allied units positioned along the border and the US Navy lurking in the Persian Gulf, Hussein could not pull his soldiers off the border or coastline. No matter how badly the war fared inland, these soldiers could not abandon their posts.

With these two simple devices, the general reduced the fourth largest army to a manageable size. Then Schwarzkopf, using tactics as old as the earliest recorded battle, rushed his mobile army in a flanking maneuver east, driving hard and fast across an empty Iraqi desert. Hussein watched only what the general wanted him to watch, the border and coastline. He never thought to watch his rear.

Saddam's defenses are rather reminiscent of Aqaba's defenses in the movie, Lawrence of Arabia. "The guns face the sea, Sherif Ali, and cannot be turned round." Likewise, Saddam Hussein's military forces were fixed south and west and could not be relocated.

In an interview after the war, Schwarzkopf spoke about his massive flanking maneuver. He said he had become nervous about halfway across the desert, because his units had met no resistance. This was nerve racking. The general thought he might have sent his army into a massive trap. Hussein could have placed a nuke or chemical weapons in their path. The American's fear was reasonable but unfounded. Flanking maneuvers were not on Hussein's mind. The Iraqi didn't even think to post a private with a field radio. The Republican Guard had no clue the American Army was even in the area until American M-1 Abrams began blasting their Russian and Chinese-built tanks. Big, big surprise.

Hussein's lack of military knowledge left him vulnerable to the superior knowledge of the educated American commander. His only military experience rested in the Iraq-Iran war, which was an unmitigated disaster.

Nonetheless, this particular group's lack of knowledge was an aberration. Most nations have some idea how to conduct combat operations. For all these country's armies, flanking maneuvers are a part of almost every battle and always have been. Alexander the Great and the Romans used them. Lee and Grant flanked and counter-flanked each other during the Civil War.

In the fight over Ramoth-Gilead, lack of military knowledge was not the problem. Both the Jews and Syrian kings knew what they were doing. They were fearless warriors, who knew how to get the best from their armies. Their chariot forces played a pivotal role in their fight, the flanking maneuver the pivotal tactic. Nonetheless, the trick worked against Benhadad, not due to ignorance, but because the Syrian underestimated his enemy.

The two Jewish kings could clearly see they had the right army and plan for victory. Without God, though, eyesight was all they had. Ordinarily, such a clever plan would have worked, which leads to the grand lesson in this chapter. Truth lies not in what we see but in what God says. We can trust our God. He will not lie.

Footnote:

1   A Handbook of Military Strategy and Tactics By Michiko Phifer, Page 74

The fear of the Lord is the beginning of knowledge, but fools despise wisdom and instruction.

Proverbs 1:7

SEVEN

BREAKDOWN OF EVENTS
1 KINGS 22: 1-28

The following is a verse-by-verse breakdown of the events recorded in 1 Kings 22 with a couple of interjections from 2 Chronicles 18. To avoid NKJV copyright limitations, this work will not quote every verse. The reader should follow along in his or her Bible, preferably the New King James Version for homogeneous communication.

Verse 1

Israel and Syria enjoyed three years of peace.

After Ahab's much smaller force whipped Benhadad

twice, it makes sense the Syrian king would have had his fill of fighting the Northern Kingdom. The three years of peace also indicates his army had not recovered from its previous thrashing. It takes time to rebuild after the loss of a hundred twenty-seven thousand foot soldiers. It's not as simple as growing and harvesting grapes.

Ahab, the victor, would have taken possession of the shields, swords, and military equipment from all the fallen Syrian soldiers. Fleeing soldiers tend to leave a lot of equipment behind too. This is a windfall, for military hardware is difficult to manufacture. Not having suffered many casualties, Ahab could find plenty of men to put the equipment to use. All things considered, it is likely Ahab's increased army now matched Benhadad's reduced army in size and ability.

Nonetheless, equality between forces creates a certain detente, for armies of equal size and ability tend to fight to a draw. Evenly matched countries tend to refrain. If, however, Ahab could increase the size of his army, he would have a distinct advantage. So, he invited Jehoshaphat to join his effort against Benhadad.

Alexander the Great used equality of size to his benefit in his first encounter with the Persian king, Darius. He lured the Persians into a tight space, squeezing the Persian frontline until it was equal to the Greek line. The terrain also prohibited the Persian chariots from flanking the Greeks. In their equality, the Greeks and Persians fought to a draw.

Verse 2

The script reads as if Jehoshaphat went to Israel as a royal visit only. After all, he and Ahab were in-laws by marriage. The personal relationship aside, the king of Judah would have known the king of Israel wanted to retake Ramoth-Gilead. Ahab's desire would not have been a state secret. Jehoshaphat would also have known Ahab had beaten Benhadad twice before. By presenting himself in the guise of a royal visit, he would have casually made himself available for Ahab's invitation to join the fight.

His automatic agreement to aid Ahab shows a keen willingness. It is also a good indicator why he would later ignore God's prophet. In modern terms, Jehoshaphat likely suffered the hot hand fallacy. Ahab won twice, so surely he would win a third time. This is unreasonable thinking, for nothing is certain but God.

Verse 3

If Jehoshaphat were coy in his approach to the situation, Ahab was doubly so. He did not address Jehoshaphat directly but addressed his own people, complaining how he wanted to retake Ramoth-Gilead. Addressing someone indirectly allows one to broach a delicate subject discreetly, expression without confrontation. Ahab may have been a rebellious, evil king, but malevolence and intelligence are not mutually exclusive.

Verse 4

Verse four is the first to characterize the nature of the battle to come. First, Jehoshaphat agrees to personally fight. He also dedicates his people to the battle, which would have included both soldiers and citizens. Wars in those days involved everyone, somewhat like America's total effort during WWII.

More importantly, the king dedicated his horses to Ahab's cause. This was a key element toward victory in the upcoming battle. The increased size in the Jewish chariot force also shaped Benhadad's response.

It is telling he committed to the fight before asking for a

word from the Lord. If he weren't already motivated to join Ahab, he would have asked God's guidance first and then volunteered.

Verse 5

So, after joining the fight, Jehoshaphat asked for a word of the Lord. This makes Jehoshaphat sound like a Godly king, but this was not necessarily the case. The king's behaviors throughout this event strongly indicate his request was due to considerations other than faith in God.

Nonetheless, Jehoshaphat would have known about the prophets who brought Ahab news of victory. No doubt, he expected a prophet of God to appear a third time with a similar report. When a prophet did not appear, he made a request.

Verses 6, 7

In response, Ahab, who also likely wondered if a prophet of God would show, attempted to appease Jehoshaphat and the situation with his four hundred Jewish-pagan prophets.

Of course, these prophets gave a good report. Everything they saw shouted victory. Nonetheless, Jehoshaphat knew the two previous unnamed prophets were from God and was dissatisfied with the word of paganized Jews. He asked again for a prophet of God.

Verse 8

" 'There is still one man, Micaiah the son of Imlah, by whom we may inquire of the Lord; but I hate him, because he does not prophesy good concerning me, but evil'. "

Elijah was still in Israel. The prophets who had previously spoken to Ahab were presumably still in Israel. A number of other prophets of God also lived in Israel. Since Ahab and Jezebel were actively pursuing and killing men of God, finding a prophet at the drop of a royal hat would be rather difficult. So, he was likely saying he has access to only one of God's prophets, Micaiah.

Now, Micaiah could not have been one of the two previous good news prophets, because, according to Ahab, Micaiah was not a good news guy. The book of Chronicles records the king saying, "…he never prophesies good concerning me, but always evil'. " (2 Chronicles 18:7) Literally translated: "…for he is not prophesying good for me but evil all his days…"

Nonetheless, Micaiah may have been the prophet who brought Ahab bad news in 1 Kings 20:35-43. The script does not mention Ahab's reaction to the unnamed prophet's bad report, but if he threw Micaiah in jail for his bad tidings, it follows he likely jailed the previous bad news guy as well. If these two were the same, and if he threw Micaiah in jail, it would certainly make finding him easy. The language in verse twenty-six certainly implies Ahab sent Micaiah back to jail.

All things considered, the two are likely the same man.

Verse 8, Continued

To Ahab's disparaging words, King Jehoshaphat said, " 'Let not the king say such things!' "

To disparage God's prophet is to disparage God's word. To disparage God's word is to disparage God. The king's admonition is good advice for everybody. Jesus said, " '…for every idle word men may speak, they will give account of it on the Day of Judgment'. " (Matthew

12:36)

Besides, instead of a prophet suddenly appearing, a pair of she-bears might unexpectedly leap into the mix and maul the two kings and the four hundred prophets to boot.

Verses 9 – 12

So, Ahab sends for Micaiah. The script reads as if the two kings then immediately donned their royal robes and awaited the prophet at the threshing floor. Although these events appear in the script as if occurring in quick succession, they would have taken time. The writers of the Bible routinely condensed events, succinctly reporting only the important bits. In reality, it would have taken a while to collect Micaiah.

Meanwhile, Jehoshaphat would have sent for his Army. Ancient armies did not move at freeway speeds. Overall, it would have taken a respectable amount of time to do all the things recorded.

So, sometime between the messengers going and coming back, the two kings sat in an area the script calls a threshing area or threshing floor. A keyword search shows the threshing floor was used for more than threshing. The writers appear to have used the word much like Americans use the word fairgrounds. Although citizens enjoy their fairgrounds once a year for fall festivals, they more often use them throughout the year for any number of other activities requiring an open space.

With four hundred paganistic prophets prophesying, a threshing floor would have had the space necessary to host the shenanigans.

The scene at the threshing floor would resemble a rally to prepare the kings, military, and people mentally and emotionally for war . This would have involved some pomp and ceremony and great proclamations. Sometime during all this, Zechariah presented iron horns to the kings, saying, " 'Thus says the Lord: "With these you shall gore the Syrians until they are destroyed". '

These horns, of course, represented the newly enlarged Jewish chariot force, the key element in the upcoming battle.

Verses 13 and 14

The messenger with Micaiah encouraged him to make his prophecy match that of the four hundred prophets. Micaiah's answer spoke a mouthful. " 'As the Lord lives, whatever the Lord says to me, that I will speak'. "

This reflects Balaam's answer to Balak in Numbers. " 'The word that God puts in my mouth, that I must speak'. " (Numbers 22:38)

Verses 15, 16

With verse fourteen in mind, Ahab asked Micaiah if they should or should not go to Ramoth-Gilead. Micaiah answered, " 'Go and prosper, for the Lord will deliver it into the hand of the king'. "

As Balaam could speak only God's words, so too, Micaiah could speak only God's words. And, as we all know so well, God does not lie.

This begs the question. Did God speak a lie through Micaiah? Did he tell his prophet to lie? This has caused a lot of confusion and likely prompted or partially prompted the mistranslation of *spirit of falsehood* into *lying spirit.*

Of course, God would not and did not deliver the city into Ahab's hand. Ahab did not prosper. Micaiah or God appearing to lie stands at odds with everything we know about faithful prophets and God. It has certainly sent commentators scrambling, each attempting to explain the discrepancy.

And, attempting to answer the dilemma through skewed logic, these commentators claim Micaiah made it clear he was not telling the truth by speaking to the king in a mocking tone. However, this is a rather outrageous statement. First, nothing in the script says he used a mocking tone. To claim such a tone speculates instead of deciphers, imagining an answer instead of discovering one.

> Many people have referenced early Jewish commentaries, which spoke of a mocking tone. This is likely where the idea originated without credit. However, like modern commentators, Jews often interjected their own ideas into God's word. Jews were not immune to personal bias, interpretation, and imaginative commentary. Jew or gentile, truth does not reside in the subjective

drivel of commentaries.

Second, and importantly, the mocking tone explanation has a major legal problem. It was against the Law to slight God or curse the king (Exodus 22:28). The obedient prophet is not going to speak in mocking tones even to evil Ahab. Good or bad, Ahab was still the king.

Many verses teach God's people to speak in even tones, even when the message is harsh. Jesus taught his disciples to " 'be wise as serpents and harmless as doves'. " (Matthew 10:16) A mocking tone is the purview of the crude and uneducated simpleton. Its use does not win hearts and minds. The one using it exhibits neither wisdom nor harmlessness.

Jude wrote specifically about the nature of speech, even condemning harsh speech in the heat of the moment.

> "For certain men have crept in unnoticed, who long ago were marked out for this condemnation, ungodly men, who turn the grace of our God into lewdness and deny the only Lord God and our Lord Jesus Christ ... Likewise also these dreamers defile the flesh, reject authority, and speak evil of dignitaries. Yet Michael the

archangel, in contending with the devil, when he disputed about the body of Moses, dared not bring against him a reviling accusation, but said, 'The Lord rebuke you'. " (Jude, Verses 4, 8, 9)

While the Sanhedrin questioned Paul, the high priest ordered someone to hit God's apostle. Paul said in response:

" 'God will strike you, you whitewashed wall! For you sit to judge me according to the law, and do you command me to be struck contrary to the law?' And those who stood by said, 'Do you revile God's high priest?' Then Paul said, 'I did not know, brethren, that he was the high priest; for it is written, "You shall not speak evil of a ruler of your people'. ' " (Act 23:1-5, emphasis mine)

With all this in mind, Ahab and Micaiah obviously had a long history. As mentioned before, the king said, "he never prophesies good concerning me, but always evil." (2 Chronicles 18:7) The king knew the prophet, and the prophet knew the king. In this long relationship, it is reasonable Micaiah always began such a prophecy by repeating the good news the king's people previously provided – verbatim. Thereafter, he'd deliver the bad.

Repeating the false prophets' words emulates Elisha telling Jehoram the Syrian king's war plans. The prophet, " 'who is in Israel, tells the king of Israel the words that you speak in your bedroom'. " (2 Kings 6:12)

An obedient prophet and follower of the Law simply would not speak in a mocking tone to his king. He may speak directly, but he will not speak insubordinately.

The king's response to Micaiah also reveals this long personal history. " 'How many times shall I make you swear that you tell me nothing but the truth in the name of the Lord?' " (1 Kings 22: 16)

This prophet and this king had an ongoing, contentious, adversarial relationship, a running theme the two clearly played out at every encounter. No mocking tone was necessary for the king to know what was what.

Verses 17 - 18

Micaiah then gives Ahab the bad news. " 'I saw all Israel scattered on the mountains, as sheep that have no shepherd. And the Lord said, "These have no master.

Let each return to his house in peace". ' "

The above terminology is not unique. Two other biblical verses use the same language.

> " 'My sheep wandered through all the mountains, and on every high hill; yes, my flock was scattered over the whole face of the earth, and no one was seeking or searching for them'. " (Ezekiel 34:6)

> "Your shepherds slumber, O king of Assyria; Your nobles rest in the dust. Your people are scattered on the mountains, and no one gathers them." (Nahum 3:18)

After their loss at Ramoth-Gilead, Ahab's people were going to be worse off than simply losing a warrior king. As a disobedient lot, unmoved by God's warnings, they were and would remain lost sheep.

It also meant Ahab would die in the upcoming battle. The king's death was, of course, a fulfillment of the previous prophecy in 1 Kings 20:42, 43. The unnamed prophet told Ahab, " 'Thus says the Lord: "Because you have let slip out of your hand a man whom I appointed to utter destruction, therefore your life shall go for his life, and your people for his people". ' "

Linking the prophecies from the two different chapters makes Ahab's response especially telling: " 'Did I not tell you he would not prophesy good concerning me, but evil?' " It is especially telling if Micaiah had given him both messages.

Verses 19 - 23

>(Verses nineteen through twenty-three records Micaiah's vision covered in a previous chapter.)

Verse 24

In reaction to the unflattering spirit of falsehood reference, Zedekiah struck Micaiah on the cheek and said, " 'Which way did the spirit from the Lord go from me to speak to you?' " In other words, my prophecy is as real as my clop across your chops. Which of us has the truth and which is speaking through a spirit of falsehood.

Verse 25

Micaiah's answer ties the previous battle's aftermath to

the current situation. " 'Indeed, you shall see on that day when you go into an inner chamber to hide'. "

By God's word, Benhadad lost the battle, and the king hid in an inner room. By God's word, Ahab would lose the battle, and Zechariah would hide from the conquerors in an inner room, either literally or figuratively. The Jews and Syrians were about to reverse roles, the smaller force wreaking havoc on the stronger by God's will.

Which way, indeed.

Verses 26 - 28

Ahab orders Micaiah to jail.

Ahab told the messenger to tell the city governor, " 'Thus says the king: "Put this fellow in prison, and feed him with bread of affliction and water of affliction, until I come in peace". ' "

To this, Micaiah said, " 'If you ever return in peace, the Lord has not spoken by me'. " Micaiah's retort is similar to Deuteronomy. Of course, the passage in Deuteronomy is a prophecy of the coming Christ, a prophet like Moses.

> " '...when a prophet speaks in the name of the Lord, if the thing does not happen or come to pass, that is the thing which the Lord has not spoken; the prophet has spoken it presumptuously; you shall not be afraid of him'. " (Deuteronomy 18: 22)

Still, Deuteronomy fits this situation. Jesus spoke only words from God. Micaiah spoke only God's words. Meanwhile, biblical history reveals a long line of men who spoke their own words. Meanwhile, too many people today attempt to replace God's words with their own. The Jewish-pagan prophets certainly attempted to replace God's words with their own. In the end, their words proved false. God's word proved true.

Conclusion

Micaiah got the last word. Before they hauled him away, he cast a final warning, "Take heed, all you people."

Yes, take heed. The people should have listened to and obeyed God. People today should do the same. Be careful when some such fellow stands and says, "I know…I know." The finite creature knows only what he can know. The infinite being wrote his words with full knowledge and foresight.

Take heed in what you believe. Take heed in whom you believe. Take heed in whom you follow. Take heed the commands you obey. Reject man's dictates and hear only the Master's precepts.

Many years after Micaiah, the council ordered Peter and the apostles to not preach the Christ. To this, they said: " 'We ought to obey God rather than men'. " (Acts 5: 29)

God's warning through his prophet is not limited to those long-ago kings, the Jewish-pagan prophets, and all Israel. His warning is good for people in every generation. The spirit of falsehood lurks in the mouths of all men. The child of God ignores what appears right and clings to what God said is right.

Moreover, the child of God knows God will not lie. The two Jewish kings did not believe God's warning, because the things they saw said they would win the fight. Likewise, when God reports some such thing in his word that seems to disagree with what we see, we face a choice: Do we believe the infinite God or our finite eyes?

The prophet did not stutter. The people should have listened and responded accordingly, even when their rebellious king would not. Likewise, God has not stuttered. We should listen to him, even when everyone else does not.

Proclaim this among the nations:
Prepare a war; rouse the mighty men!
Let all the soldiers draw near, let them come up!

Joel 3:9

EIGHT

THE BATTLE
1 KINGS 22: 29-36

Benhadad's ordered the captains of his chariots to fight Ahab only. This order is pivotal. It defines the preparation for the battle over Ramoth-Gilead and the battle itself.

As General Schwarzkopf foreknew what Saddam Hussein would do even before the war, Ahab and Jehoshaphat also would have foreknown what Benhadad would do when facing a larger military force.

In Judo, the idea is to use an opponent's strength and weight against him. The attacker lunges. The defender yields to the attack and pulls the attacker over in the direction of his lunge.

Likewise, the two kings devised a trick to use Benhadad's chariot lung against him. Rushing his chariots at a fake Jewish king of the battle divided his army. Once divided, the Jews could then surround each half with two independent armies led by two independent kings. Then, let the goring begin.

The Jew's trick was as sublime, as crafty as General Schwarzkopf inviting CNN to report on the Marines practicing amphibious landings.

Verses 29, 30

They arrived in Ramoth Gilead, and Ahab said, " 'I will disguise myself and go into battle; but you put on your robes'. "

Since Jeremiah does not mention this part until the two kings reached Ramoth-Gilead, readers have assumed the idea was a spur-of-the-moment reaction. Zechariah's iron horns show the two kings had thought of this long before they left Samaria. With the Syrian chariots out of the fight, all dedicated to reach Ahab through the frontline, Ahab's chariots were certain to gore the enemy to their destruction.

Now, the majority of English translators translated the Hebrew word, *uathe*, as *but you*, as in, "but you put on your robe." This is incorrect. Even the CLV incorrectly translates the word as *yet you*. Young's translates it correctly:

> "And the king of Israel saith unto Jehoshaphat to disguise himself, and to go into battle, `**And thou, put on thy garments.**' And the king of Israel disguiseth himself, and goeth into battle." (Verse 30, YLT, bold mine)

There is a difference between *but you* and *and you*, a negative statement instead of a positive. Nonetheless, differences, even subtle differences reshape meaning.

The translators' went with the negative, because they errantly believed Ahab was hiding from God's prophecy. Of course, he was not. The correct translation indicates a plan: I will present myself as you, and you present yourself as me.

The translators, starting their work with a false

assumption, interpreted instead of translated according to their predetermined conclusion. Predetermined conclusions born through subjective observations always produce false results. The translators should have done their jobs and left interpretation alone. By interpreting, they pawned personal beliefs off on the reader instead of producing the most precise translated words possible. The reader has an expectation of accuracy. Translating through false assumptions makes the resulting work the product of a dishonest effort.

Ahab was far from fearful. Neither king was afraid. Remember, they were the aggressors in this battle. Apprehensive kings do not go to battle with other kings. Their issue was the opposite of fearfulness. They erred by fearlessly ignoring God's word.

It took courage for Jehoshaphat to stand in the king's position as the royal bait. It also took courage for Ahab to lead a chariot attack in a battle against a deadly opponent. Notwithstanding, the translators present both Ahab and Jehoshaphat as frightened men, Ahab cowering behind a disguise and Jehoshaphat shrieking in fear when attacked.

Above all, their errant translations demand the reader

believe Ahab somehow suckered Jehoshaphat into risking his life to save his own skin. This is absurd. Nothing about their assertion makes sense. The idea a fearful Ahab could talk Jehoshaphat into putting himself in danger to save his own neck simply does not stand up to scrutiny. Moreover, a king-dependent army would never fight for a fearful king.

No, these guys were not faint-hearted, wilting flowers. Both were hard-charging warrior kings. In reality, these two kings played their roles in a well-orchestrated royal scheme to defeat Benhadad and retake Ramoth-Gilead.

Still, there are two possibilities. The two kings either devised their trick back in Samaria according to Benhadad's battle habits, or they devised it after having surveyed the situation at Ramoth-Gilead. By not informing the reader of the royal switcheroo until late in the account, the script reads as if they two devised their trick in the moment.

However, beyond Zechariah's iron horns, it is impractical to devise the plan at Ramoth-Gilead. It takes time to coordinate two independent armies for any kind of major maneuver. All things considered, it is far more reasonable they planned their trick back in Samaria. The text simply does not tell the reader until verse thirty.

> Important Note: Ahab talking Jehoshaphat into taking his place out of fear has mystified commentators and readers alike. It really does not make sense.
>
> When a passage seems senseless, in either religious or secular work, it is possible the reader has not understood the context. When facing such a thing, a reexamination of the overall chapter is in order. A better understanding of the whole may clarify the confusing part.

Verse 31

An accurate understanding of the battle hinges upon the next verse, wherein Benhadad gives his charioteers a specific, significant military command: " 'Fight with no one small or great, but only with the king of Israel'. "

He gave his order to all thirty-two captains, which constituted the entire Syrian chariot force. By sending his entire chariot force to attack the king of Israel, Benhadad, like a gambler holding what he believes a good hand, was all in.

Punching a hole in the frontline and rushing one's chariots through to capture or kill the opposing king works well. However, it is a dangerous move. First, it leaves the flanks wholly exposed (Consequently, the iron horns metaphor). Second, it wholly commits the chariots to the wrong side of the battle line. Should things go wrong, the mobile force has no latitude to save the day.

It certainly did not occur to Benhadad the Jews had set him up. Otherwise, he would have not fallen for the trick. Imagine if Darius had guessed Alexander's plan. He would have prepared his army to counter the ruse.

Imagine what Darius could have done. He could have simply not ordered his frontline to shift to his left, preventing the hole. Better yet, he could have allowed the hole, waited for Alexander's cavalry to pass through, and then closed it. This would have trapped Alexander on the wrong side of things, separating the Greek king from his army. His entire Greek force would have then moved in on the Persian frontline to rescue their monarch. Once out of position, the Persian chariots could have then surrounded and crushed them.

For the Jews, the situation was perfect. They had two kings in charge of two independent armies. Tricking the Syrians into attacking a fake king while the real king of the battle led his chariots in a flanking maneuver was a brilliant bit of military sleight-of-hand. Once an enemy army bites the bait, it cannot shake the hook. It's a death trap.

Despite God's warning, this is what ultimately persuaded the Jews to go fight Benhadad. They looked into their future, saw all the pieces they needed for victory, and went for it, with or without God's seal of approval.

Verse 32, 33

Thinking Jehoshaphat was the king of the battle, the Syrian chariots attacked.

The vagueness of these passages, especially in English, makes it sound as if the chariots wandered round the battlefield until they suddenly spotted Jehoshaphat in his royal robes. "There he is! Let's get him!" This notion does not reflect reality. The captains of the chariots would have seen Jehoshaphat, royal robes and all, from behind their own lines. Verse thirty-two simply makes the point the royal robes fooled Benhadad and his charioteers into believing Jehoshaphat was Ahab.

Now, all the translations including Young's state Jehoshaphat "cried out" during the chariot attack. Much like the *and-you/but-you* debacle, the English translators made a poor word choice due through predetermination. The thought Jehoshaphat had cried out in fear. However, it makes absolutely no sense the king would cry out in distress when attacked. He, a warrior king, was fully aware the enemy was coming for him. He was counting on it.

The Hebrew word, *zawak*, which they inaccurately translated as *cried out*, has a couple different meanings. While it can mean to cry out in fear, pain, or alarm, it can mean to excitedly herald information. In this case, the king excitedly shouted out a bit of pertinent info, something akin to, "Hey, I'm not the king of Israel. I'm the king of Judah."

The script should read, "He called out."

Now, the whole idea was to fool the charioteers into attacking Jehoshaphat as an illusion of Ahab. The charioteers were obviously fooled, so when the man in the royal robes claimed he was not the right guy, it is likely his attackers did not believe him. Yet, Kings records, "And it happened, when the captains of the chariots saw that it was not the king of Israel, that they turned back from pursuing him."

The book of Kings does not report how the charioteers realized he was not Ahab. They did not have a photograph of Ahab for a visual reference. They would not have known one king from another. In the heat of battle, all they saw was a man dressed as a king.

Chronicles provides an important detail. "…and the Lord helped him, and God diverted them from him." (2 Chronicles 18: 31 NKJV)

So, Jehoshaphat called out he was not the king, and God caused them to realize he was not fooling.

Again, the translators worked under the assumption Ahab was afraid. Therefore, they assumed Jehoshaphat was equally afraid. This is an example of circular logic: Ahab was afraid; therefore Jehoshaphat must have been afraid; therefore he was afraid. Presumption does not lead to truth.

Earlier, God did not interfere with freewill but allowed

the spirit of falsehood to possess the four hundred prophets. This time, however, God did intervene by causing the charioteers to recognize Jehoshaphat. He did something similar in 2 Kings 7:6, 7, when he caused the Syrians to hear the sound of chariots and horses. They fled in fear, believing a massive army was coming. The difference between not putting information into the minds of the Jewish-pagan prophets and putting information into the mind of the Syrian charioteers is the difference between causation and prevention.

Due to freewill, God does not interfere to make the individual or group do the right thing – causation. Man must make our own choices. He did, nonetheless, intervene to prevent harm to his own – prevention.

When the Jews sprang their trap, the Syrians would have been in a bad spot. It should not have taken long for them to succumb to the Jewish onslaught. The battle belonged to Ahab and Jehoshaphat. It was theirs to lose.

This was the outcome the Jewish kings, the four hundred prophets, and the people foresaw back in Samaria. This is the outcome they wanted. It was the outcome they believed they would achieve.

Verse 34

There was nothing to stop these two Jewish kings, nothing but one random arrow.

As the Jewish chariot forces flanked the Syrians, archers would have fired volleys of arrows at their attackers. One of these arrows struck Ahab in a weak spot in his armor, piercing his body with a moral wound. Literally translated, the arrow struck the space between the "scale-armor and the body-armor". (1 Kings 22: 34 CLV)

Ahab's death sets this chapter's ironic tone, the man's elevated hubris shattered by extraordinary randomness. To lose the battle over one stray arrow is the epitome of Shakespeare's slings and arrows of outrageous fortune.

Herein lies the core of the entire chapter. Neither the kings nor the prophets nor the people foresaw this eventuality. Only God has that kind of insight. Notwithstanding, they did not heed the warning of an omniscient God. They saw what they saw. They trusted their eyes.

Verses 35, 36

Ahab did not immediately die. His driver propped him up in his chariot, and he watched the raging battle. This lasted until evening. "Then, as the Sun was going down, a shout went throughout the army, saying, 'Every man to his city, and every man to his own country', " his death fulfilling God's prophecy in full.

In not dying immediately, the rebellious king witnessed in slow motion the fulfillment of God's word and the error of his ways. All the arrogance he had demonstrated in all his years devolved into a life-and-death struggle with one, insignificant, randomly fired arrow. He believed himself something and discovered he was but a man. And the man was unable to prevent his own death.

As he bled out, he would have suffered more than the pain of pierced flesh. He would have suffered the knowledge his wonderful, well-crafted plan would collapse upon his dying breath.

Conclusion – Faith

The kings, prophets, and people saw victory. God's

prophet foretold defeat. The Jews had a choice. They could believe what they saw or believe what God had said through his prophet.

Faith is not automatic. It is the most difficult part of obedience. Although God forbade it, the Jews multiplied horses. With God on their side, they did not need horses to win battles. However, they multiplied horses anyway, because they lacked faith God would stand by them.

Instead of exercising faith in God, Ahab and all Israel turned to pagan gods. Faith in soothsayers, magicians, and astrologers is an empty exercise. There is no power in icons, rituals, and geometric shapes. Similarly, these two kings exercised faith in their plan according to sight instead of God's word. None of this is particular only to these two kings. The Old Testament reveals a long history of God's people in both kingdoms popping in and out of faith. It's been this way since the beginning.

Jesus asked in Luke 18: 8, " '…when the Son of Man comes, will He really find faith on the land?" People mistakenly assume he was talking about the second coming. He was not. He was talking to his followers about their reaction to the events surrounding Calvary.

Events soon answered the question. When the authorities arrested the Master, the disciples fled. Upon his resurrection, he found them shattered, uncertain, and lost. They eventually rediscovered their faith between Calvary and Pentecost. But, in the moment of upheaval, violence, and fear, it vanished like a vapor.

Although Jesus was speaking specifically about events surrounding Calvary, the question stands. Upon his return, will Jesus find faith or faithlessness? It appears, he will find humanity consumed in their passions. Doubt is currently sweeping through societies like the Black Plague through Europe. Foolishly, the finite man, who sees only what he can see and knows only what he can know, says, "I cannot prove God. Therefore, he is not."

Faithlessness was a problem yesterday. It is a problem today. It will continue to be a problem tomorrow and on to the end of time. So, as every minute brings us closer to that day, the question looms. When Jesus comes, will he find faith, or will he find the entire planet heeding false prophets speaking through the spirit of falsehood?

Footnote:

1 https://studybible.info/strongs/H2199

zaw-ak' (זָעַק zâʿaq)

A primitive root; to shriek (from anguish or danger); by analogy (as a herald) to **announce or convene publicly**

KJV Usage: assemble, call (together), (make a) cry (out), come with such a company, gather (together), **cause to be proclaimed**.

About ten months ago, a report reached my ears that a certain Fleming had constructed a spyglass, by which visible objects, though very distant from the eye of the observer, were distinctly seen as if nearby.

> Galileo Galilei
> The Starry Messenger
> (1610)

NINE

GN-Z11

The Jewish-pagan prophets consulted the stars, but the heavenly bodies told them nothing. The prophets gained their only knowledge through observations. Before the battle over Ramoth-Gilead, everyone, the kings, the prophets, and the people saw the enlarged Jewish army, a solid plan, and a brilliant royal trick. The four hundred prophets trusted their eyes and said go. The kings trusted their eyes and said go. The people trusted their eyes and said go.

There was nothing wrong with their vision. The plan was solid. It would have worked. However, God saw the random arrow, the dying king, and a defeated Jewish army. He sent warning words, but they believed their eyes and ignored his counsel.

Today, when what God says in his book disagrees with human observation, the observer has a choice. He or she can either believe God and disbelieve his eyes or believe his eyes and disbelieve God. Peter saw the raging waves and stepped out of the boat anyway, because Jesus called. Gideon saw hundreds of thousands of Midianites yet reduced his army from twenty-two thousand to three hundred, because God said to do it. Years before, Moses saw the most powerful and disagreeable king on the planet. God sent him to tell the Egyptian to release his people. Everything Moses saw told him God had sent him on an impossible mission. Yet, he went by faith, because God said go.

The ultimate lesson in 1 Kings 22 is universal, good for all times in all places. When faced with a choice between what we see versus what God has said, the faithful must believe God. The faithless? They will do what they do.

The lesson is especially relevant in the information age. Science, and the stuff passing itself off as science today, often presents information in total disagreement with

God's word. For example, the universe's measurable age is ancient to the extreme, almost fourteen billion years. However, the Bible accounts for just over six thousand years of history, from creation to this day.

The difference between fourteen billion and six thousand years is like the difference between a molehill and Mount Everest. Meanwhile, as we stare perplexedly at the fourteen-billion-year-old universe, a chorus of voices opposing God and his word shout louder than ever: "Only fools believe the Bible. The Earth is far too old to be young."

On April 24, 1990, a rocket launched from Cape Canaveral into low orbit and delivered the Hubble Space Telescope. After many years searching the stars, this space telescope finally located a number of galaxies and clusters of galaxies at distances measured in billions of light years.

Galaxy GN-z11 is the farthest object yet seen at this writing.[1] This collection of stars is thirty-two billion light years from the Earth. Additionally, the light from this object, as seen from Earth, is thirteen point eight billion years old. The light does not merely appear this old. The light streaming through the telescope is literally nearly fourteen billion years ancient.

For the Christian, the difference between six thousand years of biblical genealogy and fourteen-billion-year-old light is daunting. A man with fourteen billion dollars in the bank would not notice the loss of six thousand. The disappearance of such a paltry sum would show up on his bottom line as a tiny fraction of a fraction of a percent.

The math of the stars, the same stars the ancient pagan prophets worshiped so long ago, today haunts the Christian's mind. This disparity contradicts God's word and begs the question: How does a Christian account for the difference between what God has said and the system's measurable age?

I spoke on this once in a class, and an elderly lady told me she simply did not believe the universe was as ancient as claimed. She stands as an example of maintaining belief by hiding one's eyes to reality. While denial appears to solve the problem, willful ignorance is inconsistent with logic, knowledge, and Godly faith.

On the other hand, some people have fallen victim to the math, such as the author of Does God Exist, who used to hold fast to God's word but not so much in his later years. Does God Exist is a long running series of pamphlets. The writer and writers of these pamphlets attempt to give scientific evidence of God's existence.

This was their first mistake, for we do not prove God through the science classroom but through the biblical text. For, faith comes by hearing the word of God (Romans 10:17). Without this faith, "…it is impossible to please Him, for he who comes to God must believe that He is, and that He is a rewarder of those who diligently seek Him." (Hebrews 11:6)

Faith is not proof. It is an assumption of the thing expected, certainty without observation. (Hebrews 11:1, Paraphrased CLV)

This kind of faith is not so foreign to scientists. Einstein believed black holes existed. Yet, he had only the math, which merely suggested they should exist. Nonetheless, he lived his life believing without proof. His faith was only recently proven justified.

Over time, Does God Exist shifted its position from believing God created the universe in six days to believing creation took prolonged periods of time, eons in which God created the world through some sort of evolutionary process. Of course, this twists scripture to fit what one could see instead of believing what God had said. The authors should reconsider their position, for twisting God's word to fit perception is the polar opposite of God-pleasing faith.

The answer to the problem involves recognizing the full nature of God. If the creator is eternal, omniscient, omnipresence, and omnipotence, then there is nothing he can't do. Truly, what is beyond such an entity? The question is rather rhetorical, for Jesus already answered it. He repeatedly said nothing is impossible for God.[2]

As an infinite being, he has infinite knowledge. We, on the other hand, are finite with finite knowledge. Since knowledge is infinite, and we are finite, we don't know everything there is to know. We certainly do not know everything God knows. Up until 1609, everyone thought the Sun orbited the Earth. They thought so, because it appears so. Yet, lacking all knowledge, they did not know the truth of it until the Italian mathematician built his version of Han's telescope and saw what the unaided eye could not.

So, the universe's age is ancient. We see that, but doesn't the biblical script say God created Adam a full-grown man? If so, then wouldn't Adam present with a history. For example, if a doctor were to jump into his DeLorean time machine and zip back to ten minutes after Adam's creation, he would, upon a physical examination, conclude Adam was the product of conception, gestation, natural birth, and years of growth. Yet, none of these things occurred.

> Debate rages among the intellectuals about Adam's navel. On the surface, a bellybutton in a human created from dust would seem wholly unnecessary. However, Adam was the genome prototype for all humanity. All humans, including Eve, came from Adam. His DNA is our DNA. By necessity, his genes, which shaped his body, would have contained everything we now contain, including a receptacle for the umbilical cord. So, Adam and Eve both would truly have appeared the product of conception, gestation, birth, and growth, a history that was not.

The original creator of *Does God Exist* has indicated he cannot accept the idea God could or would create a universe with a history, as if such a thing were impossible. This is a remarkable reluctance. How many times must Jesus say God can do anything before a man accepts the Master's assertion?

John the Immerser inadvertently touched on this when told the Pharisees and Sadducees, " '…do not think to say to yourselves, "We have Abraham as our father." For I say to you that God is able to raise up children to Abraham from these stones'. " (Matthew 3:9)

Consider the fullness of John's statement. If God were to raise children to Abraham from stones, these novel Jews, to be the Children of Promise, would need a physical genealogy back to their ancient father Abraham. In other words, God would have had to also create a line of Jewish ancestors back into the ancient past, people who had, up to that moment, never previously existed.

Surely, this same God, who created such a complicated universe, enormous in scope and infinitesimal in detail, can also create a universe with a history – not a presumed history but a literal history.

This is not impossible. It is not beyond an all-powerful God to create a thing both brand spanking new and ancient to the extreme in the same instant of time. "

'The things which are impossible with men are possible with God'. " (Luke 18:27)

Human senses, especially vision, are really rather limited. Due to these limitations, people must put everything seen to the test. But, the testers are limited creatures, seeing only what they can see and knowing only what they can know. So, verification does not produce an end product but simply takes humanity step closer to the end product. For instance, Galileo discovered the Earth orbits the Sun and rotates on its axis, but he did not understand everything about orbiting/rotating bodies. Humans did not come to a fuller knowledge until later, through people like Sir Isaac Newton.

God, on the other hand, is unlimited, infinite in all things. He sees what we can't and knows what we don't. Think of the difference between the finite and infinite this way. A man stands in a valley beside a mountain. He represents the finite and sees only the mountain. His trusted friend, however, stands on top of the mountain and sees everything. The trusted friend represents the infinite. If this infinite, trusted friend should tell the finite man he sees some such outrageous thing, something seemingly impossible, shall the finite man believe him or shall he dismiss his friend's report?

God stands on the tallest mountain and sees farther than any human eye. Meanwhile, we stand in the valley of ignorance and limitation. When God says some such thing in his Bible contrary to human observation, mankind chooses either to believe or disbelieve. As freewill agents, it is man's choice.

King Ahab exercised his freewill poorly and died by a random arrow he could not foresee. The person truly longing for salvation must exercise greater faith and far more wisdom.

Footnotes:

1   At this writing, the James Webb Space Telescope is in place and aligning its eighteen mirrors. When done, it will see deeper into space and with more clarity than Hubble. Nobody knows the wonders it will discover. Unfortunately, the people involved with the telescope are hoping for evidence God does not exist. Surely, they will find what they seek, for God sends strong delusion to those who do not love the truth (2 Thessalonians 2:10-13). Let's see what happens.

2   Matthew 19:26, Mark 10:27, Luke 1:37, Luke 18:27

NorDrey Books: Missoula, Montana
Nonfiction, fiction, audiobooks, and fine art photography

WEBSITE

www.NorDreyBooks.com

ESSAYS

www.RichardSpeights.com

BOOKS AVAILABLE ON AMAZON.COM
Paperback and Ebook and KDP Select

NORDREY BOOKS

Burnt Pancakes and Crummy Biscuits
The Cookbook
Patricia Ann Herren
(Available only in paper back, but also
available at BarneAndNoble.com)

Where A Wild Wind Blows
Short Story Collection
Boyd Wolf

IN THE WORKS

Propaganda, Illusion of Guilt,
and the Value of Innocence
M. Richard Speights

The Day The Elephants Forgot Themselves
Sir Pipkin Longshanks

www.ingramcontent.com/pod-product-compliance
Lightning Source LLC
LaVergne TN
LVHW051117080426
835510LV00018B/2098